YOUR SCORPIO 2024 PERSONAL HOROSCOPE

Monthly Astrological Prediction Forecast Readings of Every Zodiac Astrology Sun Star Signs- Love, Romance, Money, Finances, Career, Health, Travel, Spirituality.

Iris Quinn

Alpha Zuriel Publishing

Copyright © 2023 by **Iris Quinn**

All rights reserved. No part of this publication may be reproduced, distributed or transmitted in any form or by any means, without prior written permission.

**Alpha Zuriel Publishing
United States.**

The content contained within this book may not be reproduced, duplicated or transmitted without direct written permission from the author or the publisher.
Under no circumstances will any blame or legal responsibility be held against the publisher, or author, for any damages, reparation, or monetary loss due to the information contained within this book; either directly or indirectly.

Legal Notice:
This book is copyright protected. This book is only for personal use. You cannot amend, distribute, sell, use, quote or paraphrase any part, or the content within this book, without the consent of the author or publisher.

Disclaimer Notice:
Please note the information contained within this document is for educational and entertainment purposes only. All effort has been executed to present accurate, up to date, and reliable, complete information. No warranties of any kind are declared or implied. Readers acknowledge that the author is not engaging in the rendering of legal, financial, medical or professional advice.

Your Complete Scorpio 2024 Personal Horoscope/ Iris Quinn.
-- 1st ed.

"In the dance of the planets, we find the rhythms of life. Astrology reminds us that we are all connected to the greater universe, and our actions have ripple effects throughout the cosmos."
— IRIS QUINN

CONTENTS

SCORPIO PROFILE 7
PERSONALITY OF SCORPIO 11
WEAKNESSES OF SCORPIO 13
RELATIONSHIP COMPATIBILITY WITH SCORPIO 15
LOVE AND PASSION 24
MARRIAGE 27
SCORPIO 2024 HOROSCOPE 30
   Overview Scorpio 2024 30
   January 2024 36
   February 2024 47
   March 2024 57
   April 2024 65
   May 2024 76
   June 2024 88
   July 2024 99
   August 2024 107
   September 2024 114
   October 2024 125
   November 2024 136
   December 2024 145

CHAPTER ONE

SCORPIO PROFILE

- Constellation: Scorpio
- Zodiac Symbol: Scorpion
- Date: October 23 – November 21
- Element: Water
- Ruling Planet: Pluto and Mars
- Career Planet: Mars
- Love Planet: Pluto
- Money Planet: Pluto
- Planet of Fun, Entertainment, Creativity, and Speculations: Neptune
- Planet of Health and Work: Mercury
- Planet of Home and Family Life: Moon
- Planet of Spirituality: Pluto
- Planet of Travel, Education, Religion, and Philosophy: Jupiter

Scorpio Colors:
- Colors: Deep Red, Maroon, Black
- Colors that promote love, romance, and social harmony: Dark Blue, Burgundy
- Color that promotes earning power: Black

- Scorpio Gem: Topaz
- Metals: Iron, Steel
- Scent: Patchouli
- Birthstone: Topaz

Scorpio Qualities:
- Quality: Fixed (represents stability)
- Quality most needed for balance: Flexibility

Scorpio Virtues:
- Determination
- Intensity
- Insightfulness
- Loyalty
- Resilience

Scorpio Deepest Need: Emotional Intimacy

Scorpio Characteristics to Avoid:
- Jealousy

- Manipulation
- Suspicion
- Vengefulness

Scorpio Signs of Greatest Overall Compatibility:
- Cancer
- Pisces

Scorpio Signs of Greatest Overall Incompatibility:
- Aquarius
- Leo
- Taurus

- Scorpio Sign Most Supportive for Career Advancement: Capricorn
- Scorpio Sign Most Supportive for Emotional Well-being: Cancer
- Scorpio Sign Most Supportive Financially: Taurus
- Scorpio Sign Best for Marriage and/or Partnerships: Pisces
- Scorpio Sign Most Supportive for Creative Projects: Leo
- Scorpio Best Sign to Have Fun With: Sagittarius

Scorpio Signs Most Supportive in Spiritual Matters:
- Pisces
- Capricorn

Scorpio Best Day of the Week: Tuesday

SCORPIO TRAITS

- Intense passion and magnetism
- Strong intuition and perception
- Determination and unwavering focus
- Loyalty and deep emotional connections
- Prone to jealousy and possessiveness
- Can be secretive and mysterious.
- Tendency towards being controlling and manipulative.

PERSONALITY OF SCORPIO

The personality of Scorpio is complex and intriguing. Scorpios are known for their intensity, depth, and passion. They possess a powerful and magnetic presence that draws others in. They are highly intuitive and have a keen sense of perception, often able to read between the lines and uncover hidden truths.

Scorpios are driven by their desires and possess a strong sense of determination. Once they set their sights on a goal, they will stop at nothing to achieve it. They have a natural ability to focus their energy and are not easily swayed or distracted.

Emotionally, Scorpios are deeply connected individuals. They form strong and lasting bonds with those they care about, and their loyalty knows no bounds. However, they can also be prone to jealousy and possessiveness, as they value trust and commitment in their relationships.

Scorpios have a mysterious and enigmatic aura. They often keep their true thoughts and feelings hidden, preferring to maintain an air of secrecy. This can make them appear intriguing and captivating, but it can also make them difficult to read or understand.

In relationships, Scorpios are passionate and intense. They crave deep emotional connections and are not afraid to explore the depths of their own and their partner's emotions. They value trust and loyalty above all else and expect the same level of commitment from their partners.

Overall, Scorpios have a strong personality characterized by their intensity, intuition, and unwavering determination. They are driven by their desires and form deep connections with others. While they can be secretive and possessive at times, their passion and loyalty make them captivating individuals to be around.

WEAKNESSES OF SCORPIO

Scorpios possess a unique set of characteristics that shape their personality. While they are known for their strengths, they also have certain weaknesses that can arise in different aspects of their lives. It's important to recognize these traits in order to understand the complexity of the Scorpio personality.

Scorpios have a tendency to be intensely passionate and deeply emotional. They are not afraid to dive into the depths of their feelings and explore the depths of their own souls. However, this intense emotional nature can sometimes lead to feelings of jealousy and possessiveness. Scorpios can become consumed by their emotions, which may result in difficulties in relationships and conflicts with others.

Another weakness of Scorpios is their tendency to hold onto grudges and harbor resentment. They have long memories and find it challenging to let go of past hurts. This can sometimes create a cycle of negativity and prevent them from moving forward in a healthy and positive manner.

Scorpios also have a reputation for being secretive and mysterious. While this can be intriguing and alluring, it can also create barriers in their relationships. Their need for privacy and self-protection can make it challenging for others to truly understand and connect with them on a deep level.

Furthermore, Scorpios can exhibit manipulative behavior when they feel the need to gain control or protect themselves. Their strong intuition and ability to read others can sometimes be used to manipulate situations and people to their advantage. This can strain their relationships and erode trust over time.

It is important for Scorpios to be aware of these weaknesses and work on developing a healthy balance in their lives. By embracing their strengths while addressing their vulnerabilities, Scorpios can navigate their relationships and personal growth with greater understanding and harmony.

RELATIONSHIP COMPATIBILITY WITH SCORPIO

Based only on their Sun signs, this is how Scorpio interacts with others. These are the compatibility interpretations for all 12 potential Scorpio combinations. This is a limited and insufficient method of determining compatibility.

However, Sun-sign compatibility remains the foundation for overall harmony in a relationship.

The general rule is that yin and yang do not get along. Yin complements yin, and yang complements yang. While yin and yang partnerships can be successful, they require more effort. Earth and water zodiac signs are both Yin. Yang is represented by the fire and air zodiac signs.

Scorpio (Yin) and Aries (Yang):

When Scorpio and Aries come together, their contrasting Yin and Yang energies create a dynamic and intense relationship. Scorpio is passionate, deeply emotional, and perceptive, while Aries is bold, assertive, and independent. Both signs are driven and ambitious, which can lead to a powerful and transformative partnership.

However, their differences can also create challenges. Scorpios value loyalty and emotional connection, while Aries may prioritize individual freedom and independence. Trust and communication are key for this relationship to thrive, as Scorpio's intense emotions can sometimes clash with Aries' need for autonomy.

Scorpio (Yin) and Taurus (Yin):

When two Scorpios come together, their shared Yin energy creates a deep and transformative bond. Both signs are intense, passionate, and loyal, which can lead to a profound emotional connection. They understand each other's needs for security, trust, and commitment.

However, their intensity can also lead to power struggles and possessiveness. Both Scorpios need to find a balance between their desire for control and their need to trust and give each other space. When they learn to navigate these challenges, they can experience a deeply fulfilling and transformative relationship.

Scorpio (Yin) and Gemini (Yang):

Scorpio and Gemini have a complex and intriguing dynamic. Scorpio's intensity and depth can fascinate Gemini, while Gemini's intellectual curiosity and adaptability can attract Scorpio. They can learn a lot from each other and bring out different aspects of their personalities.

However, their differences can also create friction. Scorpio desires emotional depth and intimacy, while Gemini thrives on variety and mental stimulation. Communication and understanding are crucial for this relationship to thrive, as they need to bridge the gap between their emotional and intellectual worlds.

Scorpio (Yin) and Cancer (Yin):

When Scorpio and Cancer come together, their shared Yin energy creates a deep emotional bond. Both signs value security, loyalty, and the nurturing aspects of relationships. They understand each other's need for emotional connection and can provide the support and stability they both crave.

However, their intense emotions can sometimes create power struggles and mood swings. Both signs need to be aware of their tendency to be possessive and moody, and work on maintaining open communication and trust. When they do, they can create a loving and nurturing partnership.

Scorpio (Yin) and Leo (Yang):

Scorpio and Leo have a powerful and magnetic connection. Scorpio's intensity and depth captivate Leo, while Leo's confidence and charisma attract Scorpio. They can inspire and challenge each other in profound ways.

However, their strong personalities can also clash at times. Scorpio's need for emotional depth and privacy may clash with Leo's desire for attention and admiration. Both signs need to learn to appreciate and respect each other's individuality and find a balance between their intensity and need for self-expression.

Scorpio (Yin) and Virgo (Yang):

When Scorpio and Virgo come together, their contrasting energies create a dynamic and transformative relationship. Scorpio's intensity and depth complement Virgo's practicality and attention to detail. They can bring out the best in each other and create a partnership based on trust, loyalty, and shared values.

However, their differences can also create challenges. Scorpio's emotional intensity may overwhelm Virgo at times, while Virgo's critical nature can trigger Scorpio's defenses. Both signs need to work on understanding and accepting each other's strengths and weaknesses, and communicate openly to overcome any conflicts.

Scorpio (Yin) and Libra (Yang):

Scorpio and Libra have a complex and intriguing dynamic. Scorpio's depth and intensity can attract Libra, while Libra's diplomacy and charm can fascinate Scorpio. They can learn a lot from each other and find a balance between emotional depth and harmony.

However, their differences can also create challenges. Scorpio's desire for control and intensity may clash with Libra's need for balance and harmony. Both signs need to find common ground and compromise to create a harmonious and fulfilling relationship.

Scorpio (Yin) and Scorpio (Yin):

When two Scorpios come together, their shared Yin energy creates a deep and transformative bond. Both signs are intense, passionate, and loyal, which can lead to a profound emotional connection. They understand each other's needs for security, trust, and commitment.

However, their intensity can also lead to power struggles and possessiveness. Both Scorpios need to find a balance between their desire for control and their need to trust and give each other space. When they learn to navigate these challenges, they can experience a deeply fulfilling and transformative relationship.

Scorpio (Yin) and Sagittarius (Yang):

Scorpio and Sagittarius have a complex and contrasting dynamic. Scorpio's intensity and depth can intrigue Sagittarius, while Sagittarius' adventurous and free-spirited nature can fascinate Scorpio. They can learn from each other and expand their horizons.

However, their differences can also create challenges. Scorpio's need for emotional depth and intensity may clash with Sagittarius' desire for freedom and independence. Both signs need to find a balance between their need for security and exploration to create a harmonious and fulfilling relationship.

Scorpio (Yin) and Capricorn (Yin):

Scorpio and Capricorn have a strong and stable connection. Both signs value loyalty, commitment, and shared goals. They can build a solid foundation based on trust, mutual respect, and a shared vision for the future.

However, their reserved nature and emotional depth can sometimes create challenges in expressing and understanding their feelings. Both signs need to work on opening up emotionally and communicating their needs to foster a deeper connection. When they do, they can create a long-lasting and fulfilling partnership.

Scorpio (Yin) and Aquarius (Yang):

Scorpio and Aquarius have a unique and intriguing dynamic. Scorpio's depth and intensity can captivate Aquarius, while Aquarius' intellectual curiosity and independence can fascinate Scorpio. They can challenge each other's perspectives and bring innovation to their relationship.

However, their differences can also create friction. Scorpio's emotional depth and possessiveness may clash with Aquarius' need for independence and detachment. Both signs need to find a balance between emotional intimacy and personal freedom to create a harmonious and fulfilling relationship.

Scorpio (Yin) and Pisces (Yin):

Scorpio and Pisces have a deep and intuitive connection. Both signs are highly sensitive, emotional, and empathetic, which can lead to a profound emotional bond. They understand each other's deepest emotions and can provide the support and understanding they both need.

However, their intense emotions can sometimes create challenges in communication and boundaries. Both signs need to be aware of their emotional boundaries and find healthy ways to express their needs and desires. When they do, they can create a loving and nurturing partnership.

Remember, compatibility between zodiac signs is influenced by various factors, and individual experiences may vary. It's important to consider the entire birth chart and the unique dynamics of each relationship when determining compatibility between two individuals.

LOVE AND PASSION

Love and passion are at the core of a Scorpio's being. When a Scorpio falls in love, they do so with their entire being, embracing the depths of their emotions and desires. Their love is intense, transformative, and all-consuming.

Scorpios are known for their magnetic and captivating presence, drawing others towards them like moths to a flame. They possess an undeniable allure that can be both thrilling and mysterious. When they set their sights on someone, they pursue them with unwavering determination and passion.

In relationships, Scorpios crave deep emotional connections and profound intimacy. They long to unravel the layers of their partner's soul, exploring the hidden depths of their emotions and desires. They are willing to invest their time and energy to truly understand their loved ones, making them feel seen and cherished.

Passion runs through the veins of a Scorpio, igniting a fire within them that burns with intensity. They bring an unmatched level of intensity and sensuality to their intimate encounters, leaving their partner breathless and yearning for more. Scorpios possess a potent blend of physical and emotional desires, seeking a connection that transcends the boundaries of the physical realm.

However, it's essential to note that Scorpios can also be fiercely possessive and jealous in love. Their passionate nature can sometimes lead to bouts of intensity and possessiveness, as they fear losing the deep emotional bond they have formed. They have a strong need for loyalty and commitment from their partner, expecting the same level of devotion that they offer.

Despite their intensity, Scorpios are fiercely loyal and protective of their loved ones. They will go to great lengths to defend and support their partners, standing by them through thick and thin. When a Scorpio commits to a relationship, they do so with unwavering dedication and loyalty.

In love, Scorpios value authenticity and honesty above all else. They have a keen sense of intuition that enables them to see through facades and detect any deceit. Trust is of utmost importance to them, and once it is broken, it can be challenging for a Scorpio to rebuild it.

Love and passion intertwine in the heart of a Scorpio, driving them to seek profound connections and transformative experiences. They dive fearlessly into the depths of love, embracing the intensity and vulnerability that comes with it. For those who can match their level of depth and passion, a relationship with a Scorpio can be a transformative and unforgettable journey.

MARRIAGE

For a Scorpio, marriage is a profound commitment that they approach with great seriousness and intensity. They view marriage as a sacred union, a deep bond that goes beyond the surface level. However, before fully committing to marriage, Scorpios often prioritize establishing a stable financial foundation to ensure security for themselves and their partner.

In marriage, Scorpios must be mindful of their innate tendency to engage in disputes and criticize their partner. While their passion and desire for perfection can fuel them to seek improvements in the relationship, it is crucial for them to temper their critical nature. By fostering open communication and constructive dialogue, they can avoid weakening their partner's morale and jeopardizing the harmony of the relationship.

Scorpios are known for their unwavering dedication to keeping their marriage alive and thriving. They are willing to invest significant time and effort into nurturing the bond they share with their spouse. However, if they feel that the disagreements and challenges within the marriage are insurmountable, they possess the strength to make the difficult decision of ending the relationship, recognizing that their own well-being and happiness should not be compromised.

When it comes to gender roles, Scorpios believe in equality and mutual respect within a marriage. They appreciate a partner who shares the responsibilities of work and family duties. Scorpio women, in particular, are adaptable and skillful at balancing their professional and family lives. They strive for order, efficiency, and harmony in their marriage, approaching their marital tasks with a positive attitude and a desire for excellence.

Scorpio men, on the other hand, value their roles as husbands and fathers. They are dedicated workers who understand the importance of providing for their family. They reject sexist notions and actively participate in creating an egalitarian partnership. They are committed to ensuring that their spouse does not shoulder an unfair burden but rather shares in the responsibilities and joys of married life.

For a Scorpio, marriage is a deeply meaningful commitment. They approach it with dedication and intensity, striving to overcome challenges and keep the flame of love alive. By maintaining open communication, tempering their critical nature, and fostering equality, Scorpios can cultivate a strong and fulfilling marriage that withstands the test of time.

CHAPTER TWO

SCORPIO 2024 HOROSCOPE

Overview Scorpio 2024

As we embark on the journey of 2024, Scorpio natives will find themselves standing at the precipice of significant life changes. The cosmos has aligned in a way that will bring about a year of transformation, growth, and self-discovery. The planetary movements of Mars, Mercury, Venus, and Jupiter will play a pivotal role in shaping your experiences throughout the year. This year will be a testament to your resilience, adaptability, and the depth of your character.

The year 2024 will be a year of progress and expansion in your professional life. The semi-square aspect between Mars in Taurus and Saturn in Pisces in June indicates a time of hard work and perseverance. This period may bring about challenges and obstacles in your path, but your inherent determination and tenacity will help you overcome them. The semi-sextile aspect between Mars and Jupiter in Gemini suggests opportunities for growth and expansion in your career. This could manifest in the form of new responsibilities, projects, or even a promotion.

In terms of finance, the conjunction between Mercury and Uranus in Taurus in May suggests unexpected financial gains. This could come in the form of a raise, bonus, or even a windfall. These financial rewards will be a testament to your hard work and dedication. However, the square aspect between Sun in Gemini and Saturn in Pisces in June suggests a need for careful financial planning. It's important to avoid impulsive spending and to save for the future. Consider investing your money wisely to ensure long-term financial stability.

In the realm of relationships and social life, 2024 will be a year of deepening connections and expanding social circles. The conjunction between Mercury and

Venus in Cancer in June suggests a time of emotional communication in your relationships. This period will encourage you to express your feelings more openly, leading to deeper connections with your loved ones. This will be a time of emotional growth and understanding, allowing you to strengthen your relationships.

In August, the square aspect between Venus in Leo and Uranus in Taurus suggests a time of change and unpredictability in your social life. You may meet new people who challenge your views and push you to grow. These interactions will broaden your horizons and help you gain new perspectives. Embrace these changes and learn from the experiences they bring. They will contribute to your personal growth and understanding of the world.

When it comes to health and wellness, 2024 will be a year of focus and balance. The quincunx aspect between Sun in Cancer and Pluto in Aquarius in June suggests a need to balance your physical health with your mental and emotional well-being. This year, make sure to prioritize self-care and relaxation. This could mean taking up a new fitness regimen, adopting a healthier diet, or even taking up meditation or yoga.

In May, the semi-sextile aspect between Mars in Aries and Uranus in Taurus suggests a time of increased energy and vitality. Use this energy to focus on your physical health and wellness. Engage in regular exercise and maintain a balanced diet to ensure your well-being. This will be a time to prioritize your health and make any necessary changes to your lifestyle.

The year 2024 will be a significant year for spiritual growth and personal development for Scorpio natives. The quintile aspect between Jupiter and Saturn in May suggests a time of learning and growth. You may find yourself drawn to spiritual or philosophical studies that help you understand yourself and the world around you better. This will be a time of introspection and self-discovery, allowing you to gain a deeper understanding of your purpose and direction in life.

In June, the square aspect between Venus in Cancer and True Node in Aries suggests a time of self-discovery. This period will encourage you to question your values and beliefs, leading to a deeper understanding of who you are and what you want from life. This process of self-discovery will be a transformative journey, allowing you to align more closely with your true self.

The year 2024 will be a transformative year for Scorpio. The planetary movements indicate a year filled with opportunities for growth in all aspects of your life. Embrace the challenges and opportunities that come your way and use them to evolve and grow. Remember, the key to navigating this year successfully is balance - balance in your career and finances, balance in your relationships and social life, and balance in your health and wellness.

This year will be a testament to your resilience and adaptability. It will challenge you, but it will also reward you. It will push you out of your comfort zone, but it will also help you grow. It will bring about changes, but it will also bring about opportunities.

So, as you navigate through the year 2024, remember to stay true to yourself. Embrace the changes, seize the opportunities, and continue to grow and evolve. With balance and perseverance, you can make the most of the opportunities that 2024 brings.

Remember, you are a Scorpio - you are resilient, you are adaptable, and you are capable of great things. So, step into the year 2024 with confidence and optimism, ready to seize the opportunities that come your way. This is your year, Scorpio. Make the most of it.

January 2024

Horoscope

Dear Scorpio, as you step into January 2024, the planetary aspects indicate a month of dynamic energy and transformative experiences. You'll find yourself driven to explore new possibilities and dive deeper into your emotions and passions.

The month begins with Venus in Sagittarius square Saturn in Pisces on January 1st, setting the tone for a period of introspection and reevaluating your personal values. This aspect invites you to reflect on your desires and long-term goals, allowing you to make necessary adjustments to align them with your core beliefs.

Mercury's quintile with Saturn on January 3rd enhances your communication skills and intellectual prowess. You'll find it easier to articulate your thoughts and engage in deep conversations that lead to personal growth.

January 9th sees the Sun square Uranus and semi-square Saturn, prompting unexpected changes in your career and ambitions. It's crucial to remain adaptable and embrace innovative ideas during this time to navigate the shifts with grace and creativity.

On January 20th, the Sun conjoins Pluto in Capricorn, marking a significant period of transformation and personal power. This alignment urges you to face your fears, embrace your inner strength, and let go of anything that no longer serves your growth.

Throughout January, you'll experience a profound connection to your emotions and intuition, thanks to the Sun's sextile with Neptune on January 15th and quintile with Chiron on January 24th. These aspects provide opportunities for healing and self-reflection, allowing you to gain a deeper understanding of your emotional landscape.

Overall, January offers you the chance to delve into your desires, make strategic career moves, and explore profound transformations. Embrace the energy of change, harness your personal power, and trust your intuition to guide you towards a fulfilling month ahead.

Love

At the beginning of the month, Venus square Saturn on January 1st may bring some challenges and obstacles in your love life. It's essential to address any issues that have been lingering beneath the surface, as this aspect invites you to confront emotional barriers and work through them.

On January 3rd, Venus forms a quincunx aspect with Jupiter, highlighting the need for balance between your individual desires and the needs of your partner or loved ones. This alignment encourages open communication and compromise to maintain harmony in your relationships.

Throughout January, Mercury's quintile with Saturn enhances your communication skills and deepens your emotional connections. You'll find it easier to express your feelings and engage in meaningful conversations that strengthen your bonds.

The Sun's square with Uranus on January 9th brings unexpected changes and shifts in your romantic life. Embrace these surprises as opportunities for growth and self-discovery. If you're single, be open to meeting someone who challenges your perspective and introduces you to new experiences.

Mid-month, Venus forms a semi-square with Pluto on January 10th, intensifying your passions and desires. This aspect ignites a deep longing for emotional connection and empowers you to explore the depths of intimacy within your relationships.

On January 15th, Venus squares Neptune, creating a dreamy and romantic atmosphere. However, exercise caution and maintain clear boundaries to prevent misunderstandings or illusions from clouding your judgment.

As the month progresses, Venus trine Chiron on January 11th brings opportunities for healing within relationships. This aspect fosters emotional growth and enables you to address past wounds with compassion and understanding.

Career

The month begins with Venus square Saturn on January 1st, urging you to reevaluate your professional goals and reassess your long-term ambitions. Take this time to align your career path with your core values, ensuring that you're pursuing work that brings you fulfillment and satisfaction.

On January 3rd, Venus forms a quincunx aspect with Jupiter, emphasizing the need for balance between personal desires and professional responsibilities. This alignment reminds you to maintain harmony between your work life and personal relationships.

Mercury's quintile with Saturn on the same day enhances your communication skills and intellectual prowess. You'll find it easier to articulate your ideas, negotiate effectively, and engage in strategic planning to advance your career goals.

January 9th brings a significant shift in your professional landscape as the Sun squares Uranus and semi-squares Saturn. Expect unexpected changes and opportunities that require you to adapt and think outside the box. This is a time to embrace innovation, take calculated risks, and showcase your leadership skills.

The Sun's trine with Uranus on January 9th further amplifies your ability to innovate and make bold career moves. Trust your instincts and explore unconventional ideas to propel your professional growth.

On January 12th, Mars trine Jupiter empowers you to take decisive action towards your career goals. This aspect brings energy, enthusiasm, and confidence to pursue ambitious projects or seek promotions and advancements.

As the month progresses, Mercury's sextile with Saturn on January 18th enhances your organizational skills and attention to detail. This alignment supports you in effectively managing your workload, meeting deadlines, and maintaining a professional reputation for reliability.

Venus' trine with Jupiter on January 28th augurs well for networking, collaborations, and financial growth. This aspect brings opportunities for professional connections that can lead to long-term success and abundance.

Finance

At the beginning of the month, Venus square Saturn on January 1st brings attention to your financial responsibilities and the need for disciplined spending. This aspect encourages you to review your budget, cut unnecessary expenses, and prioritize financial stability.

On January 3rd, Venus forms a quincunx aspect with Jupiter, reminding you to strike a balance between your desire for material comforts and your long-term financial goals. Assess whether your spending aligns with your values and make adjustments if necessary.

Mercury's quintile with Saturn on the same day enhances your financial acumen and decision-making skills. This alignment supports you in making informed choices, negotiating deals, and maximizing your resources.

The Sun's square with Uranus on January 9th may bring unexpected financial changes or expenses. Stay flexible and be prepared to adapt your financial plans accordingly. This aspect also encourages you to explore alternative sources of income and innovative investment opportunities.

January 20th marks a significant turning point as the Sun conjoins Pluto. This alignment invites you to let go of outdated financial patterns and embrace a more empowered and transformative approach to your finances. This may involve restructuring your investments, eliminating debt, or seeking professional advice for long-term financial planning.

As the month progresses, Venus' trine with Jupiter on January 28th brings opportunities for financial growth and abundance. This aspect favors beneficial financial negotiations, lucrative collaborations, and potential windfalls. However, maintain a balanced approach and avoid impulsive or excessive spending.

Health

As the month begins, Venus square Saturn on January 1st reminds you to prioritize self-care and establish healthy boundaries. This aspect encourages you to find a balance between your responsibilities and your personal well-being.

On January 3rd, Venus quincunx Jupiter invites you to assess your lifestyle choices and make adjustments that promote overall health and vitality. Consider incorporating exercise, healthy eating habits, and stress-reducing practices into your daily routine.

Mercury's quintile with Saturn on the same day enhances your mental and emotional well-being. This aspect supports introspection, self-reflection, and engaging in deep conversations or therapy to gain insights and healing.

The Sun's square with Uranus on January 9th may bring unexpected shifts or disruptions to your health routines. Stay adaptable and open to trying new approaches to wellness. Embrace innovative ideas, alternative therapies, or exercise regimens that align with your unique needs.

Mid-month, the Sun's sextile with Neptune on January 15th fosters emotional well-being and intuition. This aspect encourages you to prioritize self-care practices that nourish your soul, such as meditation, journaling, or spending time in nature.

Throughout January, pay attention to any emotional or psychological issues that may affect your physical well-being. The Sun's quintile with Chiron on January 24th offers opportunities for emotional healing and self-discovery. Engage in self-compassion, seek support from loved ones or professionals, and address any underlying emotional wounds.

Travel

At the beginning of the month, Venus square Saturn on January 1st may bring some limitations or delays in travel plans. It's essential to remain flexible and open to alternative options or unexpected detours.

On January 3rd, Venus quincunx Jupiter invites you to seek a balance between your desire for adventure and the need for stability. This aspect encourages you to plan your travel experiences wisely, considering both your personal growth and your responsibilities.

Throughout January, Mercury's quintile with Saturn enhances your communication skills and intellectual curiosity, making it an excellent time for engaging with new cultures, meeting people from different backgrounds, and expanding your knowledge through travel.

The Sun's square with Uranus on January 9th may bring unexpected changes or disruptions to your travel plans. Embrace the element of surprise and allow yourself to explore off-the-beaten-path destinations or spontaneous adventures.

Mid-month, the Sun's sextile with Neptune on January 15th creates a dreamy and imaginative atmosphere. This aspect favors travel experiences that allow you to connect with your spiritual or creative side. Consider visiting places of natural beauty, engaging in artistic retreats, or embarking on soul-searching journeys.

As the month progresses, maintain an open mind and be willing to step outside your comfort zone. The Sun's quintile with True Node on January 26th invites you to embrace new opportunities and connections that can profoundly impact your personal growth.

Insight from the stars

Dear Scorpio, as you navigate January 2024, the stars encourage you to embrace transformation, personal growth, and introspection. This month provides you with opportunities to align your desires with your core values, communicate effectively, and take strategic steps toward your career and financial goals. Your relationships and emotional well-being will benefit from open communication, compromise, and addressing past wounds. Through self-care practices and exploration, you can enhance your physical and emotional well-being. Finally, travel experiences hold the potential for profound personal growth and connection with your spiritual side. Embrace the transformative energy of the stars and trust your intuition as you navigate the month ahead.

Best days of the month: January 3rd, 9th, 12th, 15th, 20th 28th, and 30th.

February 2024

Horoscope

On February 2nd, Mars semi-squares Saturn, bringing a temporary clash between your assertiveness and your sense of responsibility. It's crucial to find a balance between taking action towards your goals and being patient with the process.

Mercury's sextile with Neptune on February 5th enhances your intuition and creativity. This alignment invites you to explore your imaginative side and engage in artistic pursuits or spiritual practices that nourish your soul.

In matters of love, Venus squares Chiron on February 5th, potentially bringing up unresolved wounds or insecurities within your relationships. Use this opportunity to address these issues with compassion and open communication. The Sun's sextile with Chiron on the same day provides a healing energy, allowing you to deepen emotional connections and cultivate understanding.

On February 6th, the Sun's sextile with True Node amplifies your intuition and offers guidance in navigating your life's path. This aspect encourages you to trust your instincts and make choices aligned with your true purpose.

Mid-month, Mercury's sextile with Chiron and True Node on February 15th fosters healing communication and meaningful connections. This alignment encourages deep conversations, self-expression, and the potential for transformative encounters.

The Sun's quintile with Jupiter on February 16th brings a harmonious and positive energy to your life. This aspect opens doors to opportunities, growth, and expansion. Trust in your abilities and embrace new experiences.

Love

On February 5th, Venus squares Chiron, potentially bringing unresolved wounds or insecurities to the surface. This aspect urges you to address these issues within yourself and your relationships with compassion and understanding. Honest and open communication will play a crucial role in finding healing and growth.

The Sun's sextile with Chiron on the same day provides a supportive energy for emotional healing and allows you to deepen connections with your loved ones. This aspect fosters understanding, empathy, and the willingness to confront past pain together.

Mid-month, Mercury's sextile with Chiron and True Node on February 15th encourages heartfelt conversations and transformative encounters. This alignment enables you to express your deepest emotions and desires, fostering a deeper level of intimacy and connection in your relationships.

Throughout February, the emphasis is on emotional authenticity and vulnerability. It's essential to create a safe space where you and your partner can share your fears, hopes, and dreams. Trust is crucial during this time, as it allows you to navigate challenges together and strengthen the bonds between you.

For single Scorpios, this month offers opportunities for self-discovery and healing. Engage in self-reflection, embrace personal growth, and allow yourself to be open to new connections. The transformative energy surrounding you attracts individuals who align with your authentic self.

Career

On February 5th, the Sun's sextile with Chiron offers a supportive energy for career growth. This aspect encourages you to embrace your unique talents, confront any insecurities or past wounds, and cultivate self-confidence in your professional endeavors.

Mid-month, Mercury's sextile with Chiron and True Node on February 15th enhances your communication skills and fosters meaningful connections in your work environment. This alignment enables you to express your ideas, engage in productive collaborations, and create a positive impact through your words.

Throughout February, adaptability and flexibility will be key in navigating your career path. The Sun's quintile with Jupiter on February 16th brings opportunities for expansion and growth. Embrace new experiences, take calculated risks, and trust in your abilities to seize these favorable circumstances.

Additionally, the Sun's conjunction with Saturn on February 28th emphasizes the importance of discipline and responsibility in your professional life. This aspect urges you to stay focused, work diligently, and honor your commitments. By demonstrating reliability and perseverance, you can make significant progress towards your career goals.

During this month, it's beneficial to engage in strategic planning and set clear objectives. Assess your long-term ambitions, evaluate your current position, and identify areas for growth. With the transformative energy of the stars, you have the potential to make significant advancements in your career.

Finance

On February 6th, Venus squares the True Node, presenting an opportunity to reassess your financial strategies and ensure they align with your aspirations. This aspect invites you to find a balance between material desires and your long-term financial well-being.

Throughout the month, the energy of adaptability and flexibility will be essential in managing your finances. The Sun's sextile with Jupiter on February 16th brings opportunities for financial expansion and abundance. This aspect favors favorable financial negotiations, profitable collaborations, and potential financial gains.

Additionally, Venus' sextile with Uranus on February 27th opens doors to innovative and unconventional financial opportunities. Embrace the unexpected and be open to alternative income streams or investment possibilities that align with your values.

It's important to remain diligent and disciplined in managing your finances. The Sun's conjunction with Saturn on February 28th reminds you to prioritize financial responsibility and make informed decisions. Avoid impulsive spending and focus on long-term financial stability.

Throughout February, it's beneficial to review your budget, evaluate your financial goals, and make adjustments where necessary. Consider seeking professional advice or engaging in financial planning to maximize your resources and set a solid foundation for your financial future.

Health

On February 5th, the Sun's sextile with Chiron provides a supportive energy for emotional healing. This aspect encourages you to confront and address any emotional wounds or past traumas that may be affecting your well-being. Engage in self-reflection, seek support from loved ones or professionals, and allow yourself to heal and grow.

Mid-month, Mercury's sextile with Chiron and True Node on February 15th enhances your communication skills and supports healing conversations. This alignment encourages you to express your emotions, engage in deep conversations, and seek understanding and resolution in your relationships.

Throughout February, it's essential to prioritize self-care practices that nurture both your physical and emotional health. Take time for relaxation, engage in stress-reducing activities, and prioritize activities that bring you joy and fulfillment.

The Sun's conjunction with Saturn on February 28th emphasizes the importance of discipline and structure in maintaining your health routines. This aspect encourages you to establish healthy habits, such as regular exercise, balanced nutrition, and sufficient rest.

Be mindful of your emotional well-being throughout the month. Engage in activities that promote emotional balance, such as journaling, meditation, or engaging with nature. Prioritize self-compassion and allow yourself space for introspection and personal growth.

Remember to listen to your body's needs and make self-care a priority. By embracing transformative healing, nurturing your physical and emotional well-being, and maintaining a balanced lifestyle, you can experience enhanced vitality and overall wellness.

Travel

On February 6th, the Sun's sextile with True Node amplifies your intuition and offers guidance in navigating your life's path. This aspect encourages you to trust your instincts when making travel decisions and allows you to connect with destinations that align with your spiritual or personal growth.

Mid-month, Mercury's sextile with Chiron and True Node on February 15th fosters meaningful connections and transformative encounters during your travels. Engage in deep conversations, immerse yourself in different cultures, and allow yourself to be open to new experiences and perspectives.

Throughout February, the energy is conducive to exploration and expanding your horizons. Embrace the spirit of adventure and consider traveling to destinations that offer opportunities for personal growth, spiritual enlightenment, or unique experiences.

Be open to unexpected detours or spontaneous adventures. The sextile between Venus and Uranus on February 7th encourages you to embrace unconventional travel experiences and explore off-the-beaten-path destinations.

Whether you embark on a solo journey or travel with loved ones, allow yourself to be present in the moment and fully immerse yourself in the experiences that travel offers. Engage with locals, seek authentic cultural experiences, and allow yourself to be transformed by the places you visit.

Insight from the stars

Dear Scorpio, as you navigate February 2024, the stars encourage you to embrace transformative growth, emotional healing, and adaptability. This month offers opportunities for deep connections, open communication, and personal evolution in your relationships. In your career, strategic planning, adaptability, and responsible decision-making will lead to significant advancements. Financially, balance and flexibility are key to maximizing resources and experiencing growth. Prioritize self-care and introspection for overall health and well-being.

Embrace transformative travel experiences and allow them to broaden your horizons. Trust in the wisdom of the stars as you navigate the month ahead.

Best days of the month: February 5th, 7th, 15th, 16th, 19th, 22nd, and 29th.

March 2024

Horoscope

In March 2024, Scorpios will experience a profound and transformative period. The celestial alignments during this month will have a significant impact on their personal growth and self-discovery. The energies at play will urge Scorpios to dive deep into their emotions, confront their fears, and embrace change.

The Sun's sextile with Jupiter on March 1st creates a harmonious energy that enhances Scorpios' confidence and optimism. This alignment encourages them to expand their horizons and pursue their dreams with enthusiasm. It's a time to take risks and explore new possibilities.

On the same day, Mercury's semi-sextile with Mars sparks a sense of assertiveness and intellectual vigor. Scorpios will find themselves motivated to communicate their ideas and assert their opinions. This alignment can pave the way for fruitful discussions and collaborations.

The sextile between Venus and Chiron on March 1st fosters deep emotional healing and self-love for Scorpios. It encourages them to embrace their vulnerabilities and let go of past wounds. This alignment supports nurturing and compassionate connections in their relationships.

As March progresses, Mercury's semi-sextile with the True Node on March 2nd brings a sense of purpose and destiny to Scorpios. They will feel guided by their intuition, leading them towards new opportunities and encounters that align with their life path.

However, Scorpios should be mindful of the semi-square between Mercury and Pluto on March 2nd, as it can trigger power struggles and intense communications. It is essential for Scorpios to maintain clarity and diplomacy in their interactions to avoid unnecessary conflicts.

The square between Venus and Uranus on March 3rd may bring unexpected changes and disruptions in Scorpios' relationships and finances. Flexibility and adaptability will be key during this time.

On March 3rd, Mercury's semi-sextile with Chiron fosters deep self-reflection and introspection for

Scorpios. They are encouraged to address emotional wounds and seek healing through therapy, meditation, or self-care practices.

The semi-square between Jupiter and Neptune on March 3rd highlights the need for balance between practicality and idealism. Scorpios should be cautious of overindulgence or unrealistic expectations during this time.

As the month progresses, Mercury's sextile with Uranus on March 4th brings innovative ideas and sudden insights to Scorpios. This alignment supports intellectual breakthroughs and unconventional thinking.

The sextile between Mars and the True Node on March 4th ignites Scorpios' passion and drive for success. They will feel motivated to take decisive action and pursue their goals with determination.

These planetary aspects in March set the stage for Scorpios' transformative journey. By embracing the opportunities for growth and self-reflection, they can emerge stronger, more self-aware, and ready to embrace new beginnings in all aspects of their lives.

Love

In matters of love, March 2024 brings a mix of intensity and passion for Scorpios. The sextile between the Sun in Pisces and Jupiter in Taurus creates an atmosphere of deep emotional connection and understanding in relationships. This alignment fosters a sense of warmth and intimacy, encouraging Scorpios to open their hearts and express their desires to their partners. Single Scorpios may experience significant romantic encounters during this time, characterized by a strong sense of chemistry and mutual attraction. It is essential for Scorpios to communicate openly and honestly with their partners, as this will deepen the bonds of love and trust. However, Scorpios should also be mindful of the intense emotions that may arise during this period and ensure they maintain a healthy balance between passion and emotional stability.

Career

March 2024 holds promising opportunities for Scorpios in their professional lives. The alignment of Mercury in Pisces and the True Node in Aries ignites Scorpios' ambition and drives them to pursue their career goals with determination. This is a favorable time for Scorpios to showcase their unique skills and talents, leading to recognition and advancement in their chosen field. Collaborative projects and teamwork will also bring success, as Scorpios excel in coordinating efforts and inspiring others. It is crucial for Scorpios to trust their instincts and take calculated risks in their career endeavors. By embracing their assertiveness and stepping outside their comfort zone, Scorpios can achieve significant milestones and set themselves up for long-term success.

Finance

March 2024 presents a favorable financial outlook for Scorpios. The sextile between Mercury in Pisces and Uranus in Taurus brings unexpected financial gains and innovative ideas for increasing income. Scorpios may stumble upon new investment opportunities or come up with creative strategies to boost their financial stability. It is crucial for Scorpios to approach financial matters with caution and prudence, as impulsive decisions may lead to unnecessary risks. Seeking advice from a financial advisor or conducting thorough research before making investment choices is highly recommended. Additionally, Scorpios should prioritize budgeting and disciplined spending habits to maintain financial balance. By staying mindful of their financial goals and making informed decisions, Scorpios can make significant progress in achieving long-term financial security.

Health

March 2024 emphasizes the importance of self-care and well-being for Scorpios. The alignment of the Sun in Pisces and Chiron in Aries invites Scorpios to pay attention to their physical and emotional health. This is a time for healing and self-reflection, as Scorpios may confront deep-seated emotional wounds and past traumas. Engaging in practices such as meditation, yoga, and therapy will support Scorpios in their healing journey. It is crucial for Scorpios to nurture their emotional well-being by practicing self-compassion and setting healthy boundaries. Additionally, maintaining a balanced diet and regular exercise routine will enhance their physical vitality. Scorpios should prioritize rest and relaxation to avoid burnout, as stress levels may be heightened during this transformative period. By prioritizing self-care and addressing any emotional or physical imbalances, Scorpios can achieve a greater sense of overall well-being.

Travel

In terms of travel, March 2024 offers opportunities for Scorpios to embark on journeys that promote self-discovery and personal growth. The alignments during this month create a sense of adventure and exploration. Scorpios may feel drawn to destinations that offer spiritual experiences or opportunities for deep reflection. Solo travel or joining retreats focused on personal development and self-discovery will be particularly beneficial. It is important for Scorpios to embrace the unknown and be open to new cultural experiences during their travels. They should allow themselves to be immersed in different perspectives and expand their horizons. Traveling during this period can be transformative and provide valuable insights that contribute to Scorpios' personal and spiritual growth.

Insight from the stars

The celestial alignments in March 2024 offer Scorpios a unique opportunity for profound self-discovery and transformation. The combination of intuitive Pisces energy and assertive Aries energy invites Scorpios to embrace their emotional depths while taking courageous action. This is a time to trust in their inner wisdom and tap into their innate power. By aligning their actions with their authentic selves, Scorpios can manifest their desires and create a more fulfilling life. The stars encourage Scorpios to embrace change, confront their fears, and step into their true power. The transformative energy of this period will pave the way for a brighter and more aligned future.

Best days of the month: March 4th, 7th, 12th, 16th, 20th, 23rd and 28th

April 2024

Horoscope

April 2024 brings a mix of intense emotions and transformative energies for Scorpios. With celestial alignments influencing various aspects of their lives, Scorpios will experience significant personal growth and potential shifts in their relationships, careers, finances, health, and travel.

The month begins with Mercury's semi-sextile with Venus on April 2nd, creating harmonious communication and enhancing Scorpios' social connections. This alignment encourages heartfelt conversations and deeper emotional bonds with loved ones.

The Sun's semi-sextile with Saturn later that day inspires Scorpios to establish structure and discipline in their lives. They will feel motivated to set clear goals and work diligently towards achieving them.

On April 3rd, the Sun forms a quintile with Pluto, empowering Scorpios to tap into their inner power and embrace personal transformation. This alignment encourages them to release old patterns and step into their true potential.

Mars' quintile with Uranus on the same day sparks creativity and an adventurous spirit in Scorpios' lives. They will feel inspired to take risks and explore new experiences that expand their horizons.

The conjunction between Venus and Neptune on April 3rd amplifies Scorpios' romantic and imaginative energies. They will be drawn to ethereal and spiritual connections, seeking deeper emotional intimacy.

The Sun's conjunction with the True Node on April 4th highlights Scorpios' life purpose and brings opportunities aligned with their destiny. They will feel a strong sense of alignment and direction in their lives.

Scorpios should be cautious of potential conflicts on April 6th when Mercury forms a semi-square with Mars. This aspect may lead to misunderstandings and impulsive reactions. Patience and clear communication will be essential to avoid unnecessary conflicts.

On April 8th, the Sun's semi-sextile with Jupiter expands Scorpios' horizons and brings opportunities for growth and abundance. They will feel a renewed sense of optimism and enthusiasm in their pursuits.

However, Scorpios should be mindful of Venus' semi-square with Jupiter on the same day, as it may lead to impulsive financial decisions. It is crucial for Scorpios to maintain a balanced approach to their finances and avoid excessive spending.

The Sun's conjunction with Chiron on April 8th emphasizes Scorpios' potential for healing and self-discovery. They have the opportunity to address past wounds and gain a deeper understanding of their emotional landscape.

These planetary aspects in April set the stage for Scorpios to embark on a transformative journey. By embracing the opportunities for personal growth, maintaining balance in their finances, and nurturing their relationships, Scorpios can navigate this month with grace and emerge stronger and more self-aware.

Love

In the realm of love, April 2024 brings significant shifts for Scorpios. The Venus-Neptune conjunction on April 3rd infuses their relationships with dreamy and romantic energy. This alignment encourages Scorpios to express their deepest emotions and connect on a spiritual level with their partners. Single Scorpios may encounter soulful connections that transcend the ordinary.

As April progresses, Scorpios will experience the transformative effects of the Sun's conjunction with Chiron on April 8th. This alignment brings healing and growth to past wounds, allowing Scorpios to release emotional baggage and approach love with newfound wisdom and self-awareness. They will have the opportunity to cultivate healthier relationship dynamics and let go of patterns that no longer serve them.

However, Scorpios should be mindful of Venus' semi-square with Uranus on April 10th, as it may bring unexpected disruptions or sudden attractions. It's essential for Scorpios to navigate these changes with open communication and a grounded approach, ensuring that they honor their own needs while maintaining respect for their partners' boundaries.

For Scorpios in committed relationships, the Mars-Saturn conjunction on April 10th signifies a time of increased responsibility and dedication. This alignment urges them to build solid foundations in their partnerships and prioritize long-term commitment. It may require patience and effort, but the rewards will be lasting and fulfilling.

Career

The Mars-Saturn conjunction on April 10th brings a surge of ambition and the determination to achieve career goals. Scorpios will find themselves driven to work hard, demonstrate their skills, and take on additional responsibilities.

The Sun's conjunction with Mercury on April 11th enhances communication and intellectual prowess, making it an ideal time for Scorpios to present their ideas and collaborate with colleagues. Their persuasive abilities will be at their peak, enabling them to influence decisions and make a positive impact in their workplace.

However, Scorpios should be cautious of the Mars-Pluto semi-square on April 13th, as it may bring power struggles or conflicts with authority figures. Diplomacy and strategic thinking will be essential to navigate these challenges and maintain professional relationships.

The Mercury-Jupiter sextile on April 14th opens doors for expansion and growth in Scorpios' careers. They may receive opportunities for promotions, advanced training, or recognition for their talents. It's important for Scorpios to embrace these possibilities with confidence and seize the moment to elevate their professional standing.

Throughout April, Scorpios should also pay attention to their intuition and trust their instincts when making career-related decisions. The Venus-Jupiter sextile on April 23rd enhances their ability to attract abundance and create harmonious work environments. By cultivating positive relationships with colleagues and staying true to their values, Scorpios can create a fulfilling and prosperous professional path.

Finance

The Venus-Neptune conjunction on April 3rd may tempt Scorpios to indulge in impulsive spending or unrealistic financial expectations. It's important for them to exercise restraint and maintain a balanced approach to their finances.

The Sun's semi-sextile with Saturn on April 2nd emphasizes the need for discipline and long-term financial planning. This alignment encourages Scorpios to reassess their financial goals and create a solid foundation for future stability. By implementing practical strategies and budgeting wisely, Scorpios can make progress towards their financial objectives.

Scorpios should be mindful of the Venus-Jupiter semi-square on April 8th, which may create a temptation for overspending or making risky investments. It's crucial for Scorpios to conduct thorough research and seek professional advice before making significant financial decisions.

The Sun's square with Pluto on April 21st serves as a reminder for Scorpios to be vigilant and avoid power struggles or manipulative financial situations. They should exercise discernment and stay true to their values when engaging in financial transactions or partnerships.

The Mars-Jupiter sextile on April 19th presents an opportunity for Scorpios to expand their financial horizons. This alignment may bring a boost in income, potential business ventures, or favorable investment opportunities. However, Scorpios should approach these opportunities with careful consideration and ensure they align with their long-term financial goals.

Health

The Mars-Saturn conjunction on April 10th emphasizes the importance of discipline and structure in maintaining physical health. Regular exercise, proper nutrition, and consistent sleep patterns will be key to keeping their energy levels stable.

The Sun's conjunction with Mercury on April 11th enhances mental acuity and communication skills. This alignment encourages Scorpios to engage in activities that stimulate their minds, such as reading, learning, or engaging in intellectually stimulating conversations. Mental well-being is vital, and Scorpios should make time for relaxation and stress management techniques to maintain balance.

Scorpios should be mindful of the potential for emotional intensity and inner transformation brought by the Sun's conjunction with Chiron on April 8th. This alignment may trigger emotional healing processes and bring unresolved issues to the surface. It's important for Scorpios to practice self-compassion, seek support if needed, and prioritize emotional well-being during this transformative period.

The Venus-Jupiter sextile on April 23rd invites Scorpios to indulge in activities that bring joy and pleasure. Engaging in hobbies, spending time with loved ones, and nurturing their creative side will contribute positively to their overall well-being.

Scorpios should also pay attention to their energy levels and establish healthy boundaries to prevent burnout. The Mars-Pluto semi-square on April 13th may bring intense work demands or power struggles that could impact their well-being. Prioritizing self-care, setting limits, and delegating tasks when necessary, will help maintain balance and avoid unnecessary stress.

Throughout April, Scorpios should listen to their bodies and intuition, making self-care a priority. By nurturing their physical, mental, and emotional well-being, Scorpios can navigate the month with resilience and ensure they are at their best to embrace the transformative energies at play.

Travel

With celestial alignments influencing their wanderlust, Scorpios can embark on journeys that expand their horizons and enrich their lives.

The Venus-Neptune conjunction on April 3rd infuses Scorpios' travel plans with romantic and dreamy energy. It's an ideal time for Scorpios to plan trips to destinations known for their beauty, cultural richness, and spiritual significance. They will find great joy in immersing themselves in new experiences and connecting with the local culture.

The Sun's semi-sextile with Jupiter on April 8th encourages Scorpios to venture beyond their comfort zones and embrace new adventures. Whether it's exploring a new city, engaging in outdoor activities, or embarking on a solo journey, Scorpios will find personal growth and inspiration in their travels.

Scorpios should be mindful of the Mars-Pluto semi-square on April 13th, as it may bring power struggles or confrontations during their travels. It's essential for Scorpios to remain patient, practice diplomacy, and navigate any challenges with grace. Flexibility and adaptability will be their allies in ensuring smooth travel experiences.

The Venus-Jupiter sextile on April 23rd enhances Scorpios' ability to attract positive experiences and forge meaningful connections during their travels. It's an opportune time for socializing, meeting new people, and creating lasting memories.

Throughout April, Scorpios should prioritize self-care and maintain a balance between exploration and relaxation during their travels. Being mindful of their physical and emotional well-being will allow them to fully savor the experiences and create a harmonious travel journey.

Insight from the stars

In April 2024, Scorpios are urged to embrace transformative energies and trust the process of growth. The celestial alignments signify a period of healing, expansion, and self-discovery. It's important for Scorpios to listen to their intuition, honor their emotions, and make choices that align with their authentic selves. By embracing vulnerability and releasing old patterns, Scorpios will unlock their true potential and experience profound personal transformation. The stars encourage Scorpios to have faith in their journey and allow their inner light to guide them towards a more empowered and fulfilling life.

Best days of the month: April 4th, 8th, 14th, 19th, 21st, 23rd, and 30th.

May 2024

Horoscope

May 2024 brings a mix of transformative energies and opportunities for growth for Scorpios. The month starts with Venus square Pluto on May 1st, which may bring some intensity to romantic relationships. It's essential for Scorpios to maintain open and honest communication to navigate any potential challenges.

The Mars-Pluto sextile on May 3rd empowers Scorpios to take charge of their desires and pursue their passions with confidence. This alignment encourages them to tap into their inner strength and assertiveness, leading to breakthroughs in various areas of life.

The Sun's semi-square with Neptune on May 3rd cautions Scorpios to stay grounded and discerning amidst potential illusions or confusion. It's crucial to rely on their intuition and seek clarity before making important decisions.

May 6th marks a significant alignment with Saturn's semi-square to Pluto. This cosmic influence urges Scorpios to address any deep-seated fears or insecurities that may be hindering their growth. By facing these challenges head-on, Scorpios can experience profound personal transformation.

The Sun's conjunction with Uranus on May 13th sparks a sense of liberation and a desire for change in Scorpios' lives. It's a time to embrace their unique individuality, explore new possibilities, and break free from limitations.

The Sun's trine with Pluto on May 22nd empowers Scorpios with a heightened sense of personal power and influence. This alignment supports their ability to make significant changes and impact their surroundings positively.

Throughout May, Scorpios should embrace the transformative energies and trust the process of growth. By tapping into their inner strength, maintaining open communication, and embracing change, Scorpios can navigate the month with confidence and experience profound personal and relational transformation.

.

Love

The Venus-Pluto square on May 1st may bring some relationship challenges or power dynamics to the surface. Scorpios are advised to approach these situations with honesty, empathy, and a willingness to address underlying issues.

The Mars-Pluto sextile on May 3rd ignites Scorpios' desire for deep connections and intimacy. This alignment enhances their magnetism and sexual energy, making them irresistible to potential partners. It's an opportune time for Scorpios to explore their desires and forge meaningful connections.

On May 7th, the Sun's sextile with Saturn encourages Scorpios to prioritize stability and commitment in their relationships. It's a favorable period for solidifying partnerships, deepening bonds, and building a solid foundation for long-term love.

The Venus-Neptune semi-square on May 10th may bring some romantic illusions or confusion. Scorpios should trust their intuition and seek clarity before making any major decisions or commitments. It's crucial to differentiate between genuine connection and superficial allure.

May 13th marks the Sun's conjunction with Uranus, which can bring unexpected changes or unconventional experiences in love. Scorpios may be drawn to unique individuals or find themselves attracted to people who challenge societal norms. Embracing these differences can lead to exciting and transformative relationships.

The Venus-Uranus conjunction on May 18th amplifies Scorpios' desire for freedom and individuality in relationships. This alignment encourages them to express their authentic selves and seek partners who value their uniqueness. It's an ideal time to explore alternative relationship dynamics and embrace open-mindedness.

The Sun's trine with Pluto on May 22nd empowers Scorpios to transform their relationships and bring hidden desires to the surface. This alignment supports deep emotional connections, intense passion, and the opportunity to heal and grow through shared experiences.

Career

The Mars-Pluto sextile on May 3rd activates Scorpios' ambition and drive, empowering them to take charge of their professional goals. This alignment encourages them to assert themselves, showcase their skills, and pursue positions of authority.

On May 7th, the Sun's sextile with Saturn brings stability and discipline to Scorpios' career endeavors. They are encouraged to focus on long-term success, establish solid foundations, and demonstrate their reliability and dedication. This alignment supports career advancements, promotions, and recognition for their hard work.

The Sun's conjunction with Uranus on May 13th brings unexpected shifts and opportunities in Scorpios' professional lives. It's a time to embrace innovation, think outside the box, and explore new career paths or ventures. Scorpios may feel a strong desire for independence and a willingness to take risks in pursuit of their ambitions.

The Mars-Pluto conjunction on May 14th intensifies Scorpios' drive and determination. This alignment empowers them to tackle challenges head-on, overcome obstacles, and demonstrate their resilience. Scorpios' ability to navigate complex situations and make strategic decisions can lead to significant career breakthroughs.

The Jupiter-Neptune sextile on May 23rd enhances Scorpios' intuition and visionary abilities in their professional pursuits. They are encouraged to trust their instincts, tap into their creative potential, and explore opportunities that align with their higher purpose. This alignment supports endeavors in the arts, spirituality, or humanitarian fields.

Throughout May, Scorpios should embrace their inner power, take calculated risks, and seek opportunities for growth and expansion in their careers. It's important for them to maintain a balance between ambition and patience, as success may require perseverance and strategic planning. By leveraging their strengths, embracing change, and staying true to their passions, Scorpios can make significant strides in their professional lives.

Finance

The Venus-Pluto square on May 1st may bring some financial power struggles or the need to address shared resources with partners or family members. Scorpios are advised to approach these situations with transparency, open communication, and a willingness to find mutually beneficial solutions.

The Mars-Pluto sextile on May 3rd activates Scorpios' resourcefulness and determination to improve their financial situation. This alignment encourages them to take proactive steps, seek out lucrative opportunities, and assert their worth in negotiations or financial dealings.

On May 7th, the Sun's sextile with Saturn emphasizes the importance of financial stability and long-term planning for Scorpios. They are encouraged to assess their financial goals, establish budgets, and make practical decisions to secure their financial future. This alignment supports disciplined saving, investment strategies, and wise financial management.

The Venus-Neptune semi-square on May 10th may bring some financial illusions or impractical spending habits. Scorpios should exercise caution and discernment in their financial choices, avoiding impulsive purchases or investments. It's crucial to differentiate between genuine value and fleeting allure.

May 13th marks the Sun's conjunction with Uranus, which can bring unexpected financial opportunities or sudden changes in Scorpios' income. They may encounter unconventional income streams or find themselves inspired to pursue innovative financial ventures. It's a time to embrace flexibility and adaptability in their financial approach.

The Venus-Uranus conjunction on May 18th amplifies Scorpios' desire for financial independence and unique money-making endeavors. This alignment encourages them to think outside the box, explore entrepreneurial ventures, or embrace alternative sources of income. Scorpios may find success by aligning their financial pursuits with their authentic passions.

The Sun's trine with Pluto on May 22nd empowers Scorpios to take control of their financial destiny. It's a favorable time for strategic investments, financial transformations, or seeking professional advice for wealth accumulation. Scorpios' ability to tap into their personal power and make well-informed decisions can lead to significant financial growth.

Throughout May, Scorpios should prioritize financial discipline, discernment, and long-term planning. By being proactive, staying adaptable, and leveraging their resourcefulness, they can navigate financial challenges and capitalize on lucrative opportunities. Seeking advice from trusted financial advisors or mentors can also provide valuable insights for achieving financial stability and abundance.

Health

In May 2024, Scorpios are encouraged to prioritize their physical and emotional well-being. The Sun's semi-square with Neptune on May 3rd may bring some sensitivity and susceptibility to emotional or psychological stress. It's crucial for Scorpios to practice self-care, maintain healthy boundaries, and seek support when needed.

The Mars-Pluto conjunction on May 14th activates Scorpios' physical vitality and drive. However, this alignment may also intensify their energy levels, leading to potential burnout or the need for effective stress management. Regular exercise, mindfulness practices, and healthy outlets for emotional release can help maintain balance and prevent exhaustion.

The Sun's semi-square with Chiron on May 27th may bring emotional healing opportunities for Scorpios. It's a time to address any deep-seated emotional wounds, seek therapy or counseling if necessary, and engage in activities that promote self-love and self-acceptance. Taking care of their emotional well-being is essential for overall health and vitality.

Scorpios should pay attention to their dietary habits and ensure they nourish their bodies with nutritious foods. The Venus-Jupiter conjunction on May 23rd may enhance their appetite or desire for indulgence, making it important to maintain a balanced approach to eating and make mindful choices.

The Mars-Neptune sextile on May 29th encourages Scorpios to incorporate relaxation techniques into their daily routine. Engaging in activities such as meditation, yoga, or spending time in nature can support their emotional well-being and help alleviate stress.

Travel

May 2024 offers opportunities for travel and exploration for Scorpios. The Sun's conjunction with Uranus on May 13th brings a sense of adventure and spontaneity. It's a favorable time for unplanned trips or embracing unexpected travel opportunities that can bring excitement and broaden Scorpios' horizons.

The Mars-Pluto sextile on May 3rd activates Scorpios' desire for transformative travel experiences. This alignment encourages them to seek destinations that offer adventure, personal growth, and opportunities to push their boundaries. Scorpios may find themselves drawn to places with rich history, cultural significance, or natural wonders.

The Venus-Uranus conjunction on May 18th amplifies Scorpios' desire for unique and unconventional travel experiences. They may be inclined to explore off-the-beaten-path destinations or engage in alternative forms of travel, such as eco-tourism or volunteer work abroad. This alignment supports Scorpios' thirst for new experiences and their willingness to step outside their comfort zones.

The Sun's trine with Pluto on May 22nd empowers Scorpios to embrace transformational travel experiences. They may find themselves drawn to destinations that offer spiritual growth, self-discovery, or opportunities for personal reinvention. Scorpios' journeys during this time can have a profound impact on their perspective and overall life path.

Scorpios should prioritize safety and thorough planning when embarking on their travel adventures. Researching destinations, understanding local customs, and taking necessary precautions can ensure smooth and enriching experiences. Being open to serendipity and embracing the unknown can also lead to unexpected and memorable encounters during their travels.

Insight from the stars

In May 2024, the astrological aspects indicate that Scorpios are entering a transformative phase in their lives. The alignments emphasize the importance of embracing change, seeking opportunities for personal growth, and taking calculated risks. It's a time for

Scorpios to tap into their inner power, assert their worth in professional and financial matters, prioritize self-care, and explore new horizons through travel. The stars encourage Scorpios to trust their instincts, follow their passions, and remain adaptable to the unexpected. By aligning their actions with their authentic selves, Scorpios can experience profound transformations and emerge stronger and more fulfilled.

Best days of the month: May 7th, 13th, 18th, 22nd, 23rd, 29th and 30th.

June 2024

Horoscope

June 2024 holds transformative potential for Scorpios as they embrace change, personal growth, and the exploration of new possibilities. The month begins with Mars in Aries forming a semi-sextile with Uranus in Taurus on June 1st. This alignment activates Scorpios' desire for independence and the pursuit of their unique passions. It encourages them to break free from limiting patterns and embrace their individuality.

The Sun's quintile with Neptune on June 1st ignites Scorpios' creativity and intuition, inspiring them to tap into their artistic abilities and explore spiritual dimensions. They may find solace in creative outlets such as painting, writing, or music, which can serve as a form of self-expression and emotional healing.

Mercury's sextile with Neptune on June 8th enhances Scorpios' communication skills and empathy, making it an excellent time for deepening connections with loved ones or engaging in compassionate conversations. Their words carry emotional depth and understanding, fostering harmony and meaningful connections.

Venus square Saturn on June 8th may bring some challenges in relationships and partnerships for Scorpios. It calls for patience, commitment, and open communication to navigate any conflicts or tensions that may arise. The key is to find a balance between individual needs and the needs of the partnership.

Health and well-being take center stage for Scorpios in June. Mars' semi-sextile with Neptune on June 8th encourages them to prioritize self-care and find a harmonious balance between physical and emotional wellness. It's a favorable time for adopting holistic practices such as yoga, meditation, or energy healing to nurture their mind, body, and spirit.

Overall, June is a month of growth and self-discovery for Scorpios. By embracing change, nurturing relationships, and prioritizing their well-being, they can make significant strides towards personal fulfillment and empowerment.

Love

The Sun's square with Saturn on June 9th may bring some tests to their relationships, demanding patience, commitment, and a willingness to address any underlying issues. It's important for Scorpios to approach conflicts with open communication, understanding, and a genuine desire for resolution.

Venus' square with Neptune on June 16th adds a touch of romantic idealism to Scorpios' love lives. However, it's crucial for them to maintain a realistic perspective and avoid getting swept away by illusions. This alignment calls for clarity and discernment in matters of the heart.

On June 19th, Mercury's quintile with Chiron enhances Scorpios' ability to communicate their deepest emotions and vulnerabilities. It's an opportune time to express their needs, desires, and fears within their relationships. Vulnerability can foster deeper emotional connections and lead to greater intimacy and trust.

The Sun's square with Neptune on June 20th may bring some emotional confusion or uncertainty. Scorpios should be cautious not to idealize their partners or overlook red flags. It's essential to trust their intuition and seek clarity through open and honest communication.

Venus' quintile with Chiron on June 21st amplifies Scorpios' capacity for healing and growth within their relationships. They may find solace in supporting their partners through emotional challenges or addressing past wounds that affect their connection. This alignment encourages them to cultivate empathy and compassion within their love life.

Throughout June, Scorpios should prioritize self-love and self-care, nurturing their individuality within their relationships. By fostering open communication, practicing empathy, and remaining true to themselves, Scorpios can navigate the complexities of love with authenticity and grace.

Career

June 2024 brings significant opportunities for career growth and advancement for Scorpios. Mercury's trine with Saturn on June 26th enhances their organizational skills, attention to detail, and ability to plan effectively. This alignment favors long-term projects, strategic thinking, and disciplined work ethics.

The Sun's semi-sextile with Jupiter on June 28th boosts Scorpios' confidence, optimism, and leadership qualities. They may find themselves in positions of influence or taking on new responsibilities that allow them to showcase their skills and make a positive impact within their professional sphere.

On June 29th, Venus' sextile with Mars enhances collaboration and teamwork. Scorpios thrive in cooperative environments, where they can contribute their unique perspectives and talents while also valuing the contributions of others. This alignment encourages them to embrace synergy and create harmonious working relationships.

However, Scorpios should be mindful of Mars' semi-square with Neptune on June 29th, which may bring some challenges or uncertainties in their career endeavors. It's important for them to maintain clarity, avoid distractions, and remain focused on their long-term goals. Staying grounded and discerning in their actions can help them navigate any potential obstacles.

Scorpios are advised to leverage their natural intuition and resourcefulness throughout June. By trusting their instincts and seeking innovative solutions, they can overcome obstacles and make significant strides in their careers. Networking and building alliances may also play a pivotal role in opening doors to new opportunities.

Finance

June 2024 presents a mixed bag of financial opportunities and cautionary notes for Scorpios. Mercury's sextile with Mars on June 21st energizes their financial pursuits, providing them with the motivation and determination to achieve their financial goals. It's a favorable time for strategic planning, budgeting, and seeking profitable investments.

Venus' square with Saturn on June 8th reminds Scorpios to exercise caution and practicality in their financial decisions. They should avoid impulsive purchases or risky ventures and instead focus on long-term stability and sustainability. Patience and discipline are key to building a solid financial foundation.

Mercury's quintile with Neptune on June 8th enhances Scorpios' intuition and creative problem-solving abilities when it comes to financial matters. They may uncover innovative ideas or opportunities that align with their values and financial aspirations. However, it's important for them to maintain a realistic perspective and thoroughly research any potential investments.

Scorpios should be mindful of Venus' square with Neptune on June 16th, which may create a propensity for overspending or indulging in unnecessary expenses. They should exercise self-discipline and avoid making impulsive financial decisions based on temporary desires. Financial stability and long-term goals should take precedence.

On June 19th, Mercury's quintile with Chiron encourages Scorpios to address any emotional wounds or beliefs around money that may hinder their financial growth. By adopting a mindset of abundance and healing their relationship with finances, they can attract greater prosperity and success.

Health

Mars' semi-sextile with Uranus on June 1st sparks their interest in unique forms of physical exercise and alternative wellness practices. They may find joy and balance in exploring activities such as yoga, martial arts, or dance, which promote both physical fitness and mental clarity.

The Sun's square with Saturn on June 9th may create a temporary dip in energy levels for Scorpios. It's important for them to practice self-care, maintain a balanced lifestyle, and ensure they get enough rest and rejuvenation. Listening to their bodies' needs and establishing healthy boundaries is crucial during this time.

Venus' square with Neptune on June 16th reminds Scorpios to be mindful of their emotional well-being. They should prioritize self-care practices that nurture their soul, such as meditation, journaling, or spending time in nature. Emotional balance and self-compassion contribute to overall physical health.

Scorpios are encouraged to pay attention to their dietary habits and nutritional needs throughout June. Mercury's quintile with Chiron on June 19th supports them in addressing any emotional or psychological factors that may affect their relationship with food. By adopting mindful eating practices and seeking professional guidance if needed, they can make positive changes in their nutritional habits.

On June 28th, Mercury's square with Chiron reminds Scorpios to pay attention to their mental health. They should engage in activities that promote mental clarity and emotional well-being, such as meditation, therapy, or engaging in hobbies that bring them joy and relaxation.

Overall, June encourages Scorpios to prioritize self-care, establish healthy boundaries, and cultivate a holistic approach to their well-being. By nurturing their physical, emotional, and mental health, they can navigate the month with vitality and resilience.

Travel

June 2024 offers opportunities for Scorpios to explore new horizons and indulge in transformative travel experiences. Mars' semi-sextile with Uranus on June 1st ignites their sense of adventure and desire for exploration. They may be drawn to unique and off-the-beaten-path destinations that allow them to connect with different cultures and expand their perspectives.

Scorpios should be mindful of the Sun's semi-sextile with Jupiter on June 28th, which may create a tendency to overextend themselves or take on too many travel commitments. It's important for them to strike a balance between adventure and relaxation, ensuring they have enough time for rejuvenation and self-care during their journeys.

June also encourages Scorpios to engage in solo travel or embark on personal retreats that foster self-discovery and introspection. The Sun's square with Neptune on June 20th enhances their spiritual connection and intuition, making it an opportune time for soul-searching journeys or engaging in meditation and mindfulness practices.

Scorpios may find inspiration in Mercury's quintile with Neptune on June 8th, which supports them in connecting with locals and immersing themselves in the cultural richness of their destinations. They may have profound encounters or gain valuable insights through their interactions with different communities.

Traveling during June offers Scorpios the chance to rejuvenate their spirits, gain new perspectives, and broaden their horizons. It's essential for them to embrace flexibility, practice mindfulness, and embrace the transformative potential that travel brings.

Insight from the stars

June 2024 invites Scorpios to embrace transformation, prioritize self-care, and nurture their connections. The alignments indicate potential challenges in relationships and finances, requiring patience and open communication. However, opportunities for growth and success are abundant in their careers, health, and travels. By staying grounded, trusting their intuition, and focusing on long-term goals, Scorpios can overcome obstacles and make significant strides. It's important for them to listen to their bodies, practice self-compassion, and find balance in their pursuit of personal and professional aspirations. Embracing change with grace and authenticity will lead to transformative outcomes.

Best days of the month: June 2nd, 8th,13th, 17th, 21st, 26th 29th

July 2024

Horoscope

July 2024 is a month of profound transformation and growth for Scorpios. As the Sun moves through Cancer, the sign preceding Scorpio, it illuminates the deeper layers of the Scorpio psyche, encouraging self-reflection and introspection. The planetary aspects during this period indicate a time of intense emotions, significant shifts, and powerful opportunities for personal evolution.

At the beginning of the month, on July 1st, Jupiter in Gemini forms a semi-square with Chiron in Aries. This aspect brings to light any unresolved wounds or deep-seated insecurities that Scorpios may carry within themselves. It prompts them to confront their vulnerabilities and engage in healing work to find emotional wholeness.

Mercury's quintile with Mars on the same day amplifies Scorpios' mental acuity and assertiveness.

They possess a sharp intellect and the ability to effectively communicate their ideas and desires. This aspect empowers Scorpios to express themselves with confidence and assert their needs in various areas of life.

As the month progresses, the Sun in Cancer semi-squares Uranus in Taurus on July 1st, generating an air of unpredictability and restlessness. Scorpios may experience sudden changes or disruptions in their routines, which can be both challenging and invigorating. It is crucial for Scorpios to embrace flexibility and adaptability during this period.

On July 2nd, Mercury forms a harmonious trine with Neptune in Pisces, heightening Scorpios' intuition and imaginative abilities. They have a heightened sensitivity to subtle energies and can tap into their creative potential. This aspect is favorable for artistic pursuits, spiritual practices, and deepening emotional connections with others.

However, the Sun's square with the True Node on the same day presents a cosmic challenge for Scorpios. It urges them to reassess their life direction and make necessary adjustments to align with their true purpose. Scorpios may feel a sense of conflict between their past patterns and the path they aspire to follow. This square invites them to release old patterns and embrace a new trajectory that is more authentic and aligned with their soul's journey.

Throughout the month, Scorpios may encounter various planetary aspects that highlight the importance of addressing emotional wounds and engaging in inner healing. The opposition between Mercury and Pluto on July 3rd indicates the need to confront deep-rooted fears, psychological patterns, or power struggles that may hinder personal growth. It is essential for Scorpios to delve into their subconscious and engage in therapeutic practices to bring about profound transformation.

Love

The month of July brings a deep exploration of love and relationships for Scorpios. With Jupiter semi-square Chiron in the early days of the month, there may be some healing work required in romantic partnerships. However, Mercury's quintile with Mars on July 1st fosters open and honest communication, allowing Scorpios to express their desires and concerns. As the month progresses, the trine between Mercury and Neptune on July 2nd enhances emotional connection and understanding. Scorpios may find themselves drawn to spiritual or artistic pursuits with their partners, deepening the bond. The Sun's square with the True Node on July 2nd brings some challenges, urging Scorpios to reassess their relationship goals and make necessary adjustments. Venus trine Saturn on July 2nd provides stability and commitment, enabling Scorpios to build a solid foundation in their relationships. Towards the end of the month, Venus's opposition to Pluto on July 12th may bring intense power struggles or transformative experiences in love. It is essential for Scorpios to confront any underlying issues and work towards healing and growth.

Career

Scorpios' career prospects in July 2024 show promise, but not without some hurdles. The opposition between Mercury and Pluto on July 3rd signals potential power struggles or conflicts with colleagues or superiors. It is crucial for Scorpios to maintain diplomacy and find ways to resolve conflicts amicably. However, the sextile between Mars and Saturn on July 5th provides the determination and discipline necessary to overcome obstacles and achieve professional goals. Scorpios may find that their perseverance pays off, as indicated by the sextile between Venus and Uranus on July 8th, bringing unexpected opportunities or favorable circumstances in their career. The sextile between Jupiter and the True Node on July 9th encourages Scorpios to expand their professional network and seek collaborative projects. Additionally, Mercury's sextile with Jupiter on July 8th enhances communication skills, making it easier for Scorpios to convey their ideas and gain support from others. It is essential for Scorpios to stay focused, adaptable, and open to new possibilities, as success lies in their ability to navigate through challenges.

Finance

July 2024 holds mixed prospects for Scorpio's financial matters. With the square between Venus and Chiron on July 6th, Scorpios may need to address past financial wounds or issues that have been affecting their current situation. However, the trine between Venus and Saturn on July 8th brings stability and the potential for financial gain through disciplined and strategic planning. It is a favorable time for long-term investments or financial collaborations. The sextile between Venus and Uranus on July 18th may bring unexpected financial opportunities or windfalls. Scorpios should remain cautious and make informed decisions to make the most of these favorable alignments. It is advisable to seek professional advice and manage resources wisely to maintain financial stability throughout the month.

Health

Scorpios' physical and emotional well-being require attention in July 2024. The semi-square between the Sun and Uranus on July 1st may bring unexpected disruptions or changes in their daily routines, which can impact their overall health. It is crucial for Scorpios to maintain a balanced lifestyle and prioritize self-care practices. The square between the Sun and Chiron on July 15th may bring emotional healing opportunities, prompting Scorpios to confront deep-seated emotional issues that may be affecting their well-being. Seeking support from therapists or engaging in activities such as meditation, yoga, or counseling can assist in the healing process. Additionally, Mars' conjunction with Uranus on July

15th urges Scorpios to channel their energy and aggression in constructive ways to avoid unnecessary physical or emotional stress. Prioritizing rest, adopting healthy habits, and practicing mindfulness will contribute to Scorpios' overall well-being throughout the month.

Travel

July 2024 presents opportunities for Scorpios to embark on transformative journeys, both physically and metaphorically. The trine between Venus and Neptune on July 11th ignites a sense of adventure and wanderlust. It is an ideal time for Scorpios to plan trips that allow them to explore new cultures, expand their horizons, and gain spiritual insights. Whether it's a solo trip or with loved ones, these experiences will leave a profound impact on Scorpios' personal growth and perspective. However, it is crucial for Scorpios to remain cautious during their travels, as the square between Mercury and Uranus on July 21st may bring unexpected disruptions or challenges. Planning ahead, staying flexible, and maintaining open communication will help Scorpios navigate any travel-related obstacles.

Insight from the stars

The celestial alignments in July 2024 provide Scorpios with opportunities for transformation, growth, and self-discovery. While challenges may arise in various areas of life, they serve as catalysts for personal and professional development. The planetary configurations encourage Scorpios to confront their fears, heal emotional wounds, and embrace change. By maintaining a balanced approach, harnessing their determination, and seeking support when needed, Scorpios can navigate the month with resilience and come out stronger. The insights gained during this period will lay the foundation for future success and fulfillment. Trusting the journey and aligning with the cosmic energies will enable Scorpios to embrace their true potential and manifest their desires.

Best days of the month: July 2nd, 8th, 9th, 11th, 18th, 21st and 31st.

August 2024

Horoscope

August 2024 marks a transformative period for Scorpios as they navigate intense cosmic energies and embark on a journey of self-discovery and growth. With powerful planetary aspects, this month presents Scorpios with opportunities for profound personal transformation in all aspects of their lives. The celestial alignments encourage Scorpios to delve deep within themselves, confront their fears, and embrace change to manifest their true desires.

The month begins with Mars sextile True Node on August 1st, igniting a sense of purpose and direction. Scorpios feel driven to align their actions with their soul's path, propelling them towards growth and fulfillment. This aspect empowers Scorpios to take decisive action, forge new connections, and embrace opportunities that contribute to their overall development.

Throughout August, Scorpios are urged to find a balance between their personal desires and responsibilities in their careers. The conjunction between Mars and Jupiter on August 14th ignites Scorpios' ambition and drive for success. They are motivated to expand their horizons, take calculated risks, and pursue their professional goals with passion and determination.

Scorpios are encouraged to prioritize self-care and emotional well-being. The intense energies of this month may take a toll on their physical and mental health. It is important for Scorpios to establish healthy routines, engage in stress-reducing activities, and seek support when needed. By nurturing their well-being, Scorpios can maintain balance and navigate the transformative energies of the month with resilience and strength.

Love

Mars forms a sextile with the True Node on August 1st, enhancing Scorpios' intuition and ability to navigate their relationships with clarity. They have a keen sense of what they desire in a partnership and can make decisions that align with their emotional needs. However, the semi-square between Mars and Chiron on the same day may bring moments of vulnerability or past wounds resurfacing. It is crucial for Scorpios to address any emotional healing that is required to create a solid foundation for their love life.

Venus quintile Jupiter on August 2nd ignites a sense of optimism and expansion in romantic connections. Scorpios may experience moments of joy and connection with their partners. However, Venus's square with Uranus on the same day introduces an element of unpredictability and potential disruptions in relationships. It is important for Scorpios to maintain open communication and flexibility to navigate these challenges.

Throughout the month, Scorpios are urged to find a balance between their own individuality and the needs of their partners. The quincunx aspect between Venus and Neptune on August 4th may bring some confusion or misunderstandings in love. Clear communication and emotional attunement will be essential to maintain harmony. The biquintile between Venus and True Node on August 6th presents opportunities for growth and evolution in relationships. Scorpios may find themselves drawn to partners who support their personal development and align with their life purpose.

Career

August 2024 presents both opportunities and obstacles in Scorpios' professional lives. The conjunction between Mars and Jupiter on August 14th infuses Scorpios with enthusiasm, ambition, and the drive to pursue their career goals. They possess a strong desire for growth and are willing to put in the necessary effort to achieve success. However, the square between Mars and Saturn on August 16th may bring some challenges or resistance from authority figures or colleagues. It is important for Scorpios to remain patient, focused, and adaptable in the face of setbacks. Through determination and strategic planning, they can overcome these obstacles and make significant progress.

Scorpios are encouraged to tap into their intuition and leverage their intellectual prowess in the workplace. The trine between Mercury and Chiron on August 23rd enhances their ability to communicate effectively and empathetically, fostering harmonious relationships with colleagues and superiors. Collaboration and seeking support from trusted allies will be beneficial for Scorpios' career advancement.

Finance

Financial matters in August 2024 require careful attention and planning for Scorpios. The quincunx aspect between Venus and Jupiter on August 19th may create some financial challenges or unexpected expenses. It is important for Scorpios to exercise prudence and avoid impulsive spending during this time. The opposition between Venus and Saturn on the same day emphasizes the need for discipline, responsibility, and long-term financial planning. By adopting a cautious approach and avoiding unnecessary risks, Scorpios can maintain financial stability.

However, opportunities for financial growth and abundance are also present. The trine between Venus and Uranus on August 27th brings unexpected financial gains or innovative ideas for increasing income. Scorpios may find success by exploring unconventional avenues or embracing their unique talents and skills. Seeking professional advice and developing a strategic financial plan will maximize these opportunities.

Health

August 2024 highlights the importance of self-care and emotional well-being for Scorpios. The intense energies of the month may impact their physical and mental health. The sesquiquadrate aspect between the Sun and Neptune on August 6th may create moments of confusion or emotional sensitivity. It is crucial for Scorpios to prioritize self-care practices such as meditation, relaxation techniques, and seeking emotional support when needed.

The square between the Sun and Uranus on August 19th may introduce sudden disruptions or changes in routine, which can lead to increased stress levels. It is essential for Scorpios to maintain a balanced lifestyle, prioritize rest, and engage in activities that promote relaxation and mental clarity. Listening to their bodies' needs and practicing self-compassion will contribute to their overall well-being.

Travel

August 2024 offers opportunities for transformative travel experiences for Scorpios. The quincunx aspect between Venus and Chiron on August 23rd may inspire them to embark on a journey of self-discovery and healing. Whether it is a solo adventure or accompanied by loved ones, travel during this time can bring profound insights and personal growth. Scorpios are advised to embrace spontaneity and explore destinations that align with their spiritual or cultural interests. However, it is essential to remain flexible and open to unexpected changes or challenges that may arise during travel.

Insight from the stars

The celestial alignments in August 2024 present Scorpios with a powerful period of personal transformation and growth. The intense emotions and challenges they encounter serve as catalysts for their evolution. The key to navigating this transformative journey lies in self-reflection, healing past wounds, and embracing change. By tapping into their intuition, communicating effectively, and cultivating self-care practices, Scorpios can harness the cosmic energies to manifest their desires and fulfill their true potential.

Best days of the month: August 2nd, 14th, 15th, 23rd, 27th, 29th and 30th.

September 2024

Horoscope

September 2024 brings a transformative and eventful month for Scorpios. The celestial alignments and planetary aspects indicate that significant shifts and opportunities await you in various aspects of your life. It is a period of growth, self-reflection, and embracing new beginnings. During this time, you are encouraged to delve deep into your emotions, confront your fears, and let go of old patterns that no longer serve your highest good.

The planetary configurations in September will guide you towards tapping into your inner strength and resilience. By embracing these energies, you can navigate the changes and challenges that come your way and create the life you truly desire.

This month is ideal for self-exploration and self-discovery. Take the time to reflect on your past experiences and the lessons they have taught you. This introspection will provide valuable insights that will assist you in making important decisions and taking proactive steps towards your goals.

Emotional healing and personal growth will be significant themes during September. The alignment of Mercury trine Chiron on September 2nd will support deep emotional healing and help you address any emotional wounds that may be holding you back. It is a time to release old emotional baggage and embrace a renewed sense of self.

As the Sun quintiles Mars on September 2nd, you will feel a surge of motivation and assertiveness. This aspect empowers you to take charge of your life and assert yourself confidently. Use this energy to pursue your passions and take bold action towards your goals.

Overall, September holds immense potential for Scorpios to embark on a transformative journey. By embracing the shifts, cultivating self-reflection, and harnessing your inner strength, you can navigate the changes ahead and create a life filled with fulfillment and growth.

Love

Love takes center stage for Scorpios in September 2024, as the planetary aspects and alignments bring forth opportunities for deep connections, growth, and transformation in relationships.

The trine between Venus and Jupiter on September 15th creates an atmosphere of love, harmony, and expansion. This aspect brings positive energy to your romantic relationships, fostering a sense of joy, generosity, and emotional fulfillment. It's a wonderful time to strengthen bonds, express love and affection, and create memorable experiences with your partner.

The opposition between Venus and Chiron on September 16th may bring emotional healing and growth in relationships. This aspect invites you to confront any unresolved wounds or insecurities, both individually and as a couple. By addressing these vulnerabilities with empathy and compassion, you can strengthen the foundation of your relationship and foster a deeper level of intimacy and trust.

The Venus opposition to Neptune on September 21st calls for clarity and discernment in matters of the heart. It's important to avoid idealizing relationships or getting swept away by unrealistic expectations. Stay grounded and ensure that your romantic pursuits align with your values and long-term goals. Trust your intuition to guide you in making wise decisions regarding love and partnerships.

For single Scorpios, the biquintile between Venus and Uranus on September 15th sparks excitement and the potential for unexpected romantic encounters. Be open to new experiences and allow yourself to step out of your comfort zone. This aspect encourages you to embrace spontaneity and explore connections that may bring surprises and personal growth.

Communication plays a vital role in relationships, and the Mercury quintile Mars on September 21st amplifies your ability to express your desires, needs, and emotions effectively. Use this energy to engage in meaningful conversations, resolve conflicts, and deepen emotional bonds with your loved ones.

Career

In the realm of career and professional endeavors, September brings transformative energy and opportunities for Scorpios. The planetary aspects and alignments indicate that it is a time of significant growth and advancement in your professional life.

The alignment of Mercury trine Pluto on September 26th empowers you with strong communication skills and the ability to influence others. This aspect enhances your problem-solving abilities and allows you to make persuasive arguments and decisions. Use this powerful energy to collaborate effectively, negotiate deals, or present innovative ideas in the workplace.

The biquintile between Mercury and Neptune on September 2nd stimulates your creativity and intuition. You may find yourself drawn to unconventional approaches or innovative solutions in your career. Trust your instincts and think outside the box to make a positive impact and stand out from the crowd.

Additionally, the quintile between Mercury and Mars on September 21st further amplifies your mental acuity and assertiveness. This aspect enhances your strategic thinking and provides the drive necessary to take decisive action. You may find yourself taking on leadership roles or initiating new projects that showcase your capabilities.

However, it is essential to be cautious of the Mercury square Jupiter aspect on September 21st, as it may lead to overconfidence or impulsiveness. Take the time to carefully evaluate your options and consider the long-term consequences before making any major decisions.

Finance

September brings a mix of opportunities and challenges in the realm of finances for Scorpios. The planetary aspects and alignments indicate that it is a time to carefully evaluate your financial situation, make strategic decisions, and exercise caution.

The sesquiquadrate between Venus and Uranus on September 8th may bring unexpected expenses or fluctuations in income. It is crucial to stay vigilant and maintain a balanced approach to your finances. Consider creating a budget or revisiting your financial goals to ensure stability and adaptability in the face of any financial surprises.

The trine between Venus and Jupiter on September 15th brings a positive influence on your financial endeavors. This aspect signifies potential abundance, growth, and opportunities for financial expansion. You may receive favorable financial news or experience an increase in income. However, it is important to manage your resources wisely and avoid excessive spending or impulsive investments.

The opposition between Venus and Chiron on September 16th emphasizes the need for emotional awareness and healing in relation to your financial well-being. Take time to address any limiting beliefs or emotional patterns that may be impacting your financial decisions. Cultivate a healthy mindset towards money and abundance to attract positive financial outcomes.

To maximize financial success, utilize the analytical skills and attention to detail granted by the Mercury opposition to Neptune on September 25th. This aspect supports careful financial planning, meticulous budgeting, and thorough research before making any major financial decisions or investments.

Health

The month of September brings a focus on health and well-being for Scorpios. The planetary aspects and alignments indicate the importance of taking care of your physical, mental, and emotional well-being during this time.

The sesquiquadrate between the Sun and Pluto on September 6th may bring intense energy and the potential for power struggles. It is crucial to manage stress levels and practice self-care to avoid any negative impact on your health. Engage in activities that promote relaxation and balance, such as meditation, yoga, or spending time in nature.

The trine between the Sun and Uranus on September 19th offers a burst of energy and vitality. This aspect can inspire you to try new exercise routines or embark on health-related projects. Embrace this opportunity to introduce positive lifestyle changes, such as incorporating regular physical activity, adopting a nutritious diet, and prioritizing adequate rest and sleep.

The quincunx between Mercury and Chiron on September 21st highlights the importance of maintaining emotional well-being as it directly affects your overall health. Take time for self-reflection and seek support from loved ones or a therapist if needed. Nurture your emotional health through practices like journaling, mindfulness, or engaging in activities that bring you joy.

The opposition between Mercury and Neptune on September 25th may bring a need for clear communication and accurate information regarding your health. Be cautious of misinformation or misdiagnoses, and seek professional advice when necessary. It is a good time to schedule medical check-ups and address any lingering health concerns.

Travel

September presents opportunities for travel and exploration for Scorpios. Whether it's a short getaway or a long-distance journey, the planetary aspects and alignments suggest that travel can be enriching and transformative during this time.

The biquintile between Venus and Uranus on September 15th sparks a sense of adventure and a desire for new experiences. It may inspire you to embark on spontaneous trips or explore unfamiliar destinations. Embrace the excitement of discovering new cultures, cuisines, and perspectives as you expand your horizons through travel.

The quincunx between Venus and Neptune on September 21st advises caution when it comes to travel arrangements and logistics. Double-check your itineraries, ensure you have all necessary documents, and be mindful of any potential delays or miscommunications. Planning ahead and staying organized will help you avoid unnecessary stress during your travels.

For those considering business-related trips or networking opportunities, the Mercury quintile Mars on September 21st enhances your communication and negotiation skills. This aspect supports successful meetings, conferences, and collaborations. Take advantage of this favorable energy to build new connections and make a lasting impression in your professional endeavors.

When traveling, it is essential to prioritize your well-being. The Sun opposition to Neptune on September 20th reminds you to listen to your body's needs and practice self-care during your journeys. Take breaks, stay hydrated, and prioritize restful sleep to ensure you have the energy to fully enjoy your travel experiences.

If international travel is on your agenda, be aware of any travel advisories or restrictions due to the current global climate. Stay informed about health and safety protocols, and take necessary precautions to protect yourself and others.

Insight from the stars

The celestial alignments in September indicate a period of transformation and growth for Scorpios. The combination of planetary aspects highlights the importance of embracing change, self-reflection, and taking courageous steps towards your goals. Trust your intuition and inner wisdom as you navigate the opportunities and challenges that arise. This month offers a powerful energetic shift, allowing you to tap into your innate strength and resilience. Embrace the transformative energies and let the stars guide you towards self-discovery, personal evolution, and a renewed sense of purpose. By aligning with the cosmic flow, you can manifest positive changes and create a fulfilling life path.

Best days of the month: September 3rd, 15th, 19th, 22nd, 25th, 26th, and 30th.

October 2024

Horoscope

October 2024 brings a powerful and transformative energy for Scorpios, influenced by the astrological aspects. The sesquiquadrate between Mercury in Libra and Uranus in Taurus on October 2nd highlights the need for mental flexibility and adaptability. This aspect encourages you to embrace new ideas and innovative approaches.

As Mercury forms a semi-sextile with Venus in Scorpio on October 3rd, your communication skills are enhanced, allowing for meaningful and intimate conversations in your relationships. This is an opportune time to express your emotions and deepen your connections.

Venus, the planet of love and harmony, forms a biquintile with the True Node on October 3rd, encouraging you to align your romantic pursuits with your higher purpose. This aspect inspires you to seek relationships that support your personal growth and spiritual journey.

The sesquiquadrate between Venus in Scorpio and Neptune in Pisces on October 3rd can bring a sense of idealism and sensitivity to your love life. Be mindful of potential illusions or unrealistic expectations, and ensure that you maintain healthy boundaries.

In the realm of career, the quincunx aspect between Mercury in Libra and Saturn in Pisces on October 4th urges you to find a balance between your professional responsibilities and your need for personal fulfillment. It may require adjustments and careful planning to achieve this equilibrium.

The sesquiquadrate between the Sun in Libra and Uranus in Taurus on October 4th brings unexpected changes and opportunities in your career. Embrace the element of surprise and be open to new paths and possibilities.

With Venus trine Saturn on October 4th, your dedication and hard work in your professional endeavors are recognized and rewarded. This aspect enhances your reputation and supports your long-term goals.

Love

In October 2024, love takes on a passionate and transformative tone for Scorpios, thanks to the astrological aspects. Venus's entrance into Scorpio on October 22nd intensifies your magnetism and allure, making you irresistible to others. This transit sparks deep emotional connections and brings forth profound experiences in your relationships.

The trine between Venus in Scorpio and Saturn in Pisces on October 4th provides stability and commitment in your love life. You and your partner may strengthen your bond through shared responsibilities and mutual support. This aspect fosters trust and deepens your connection, making it an ideal time for serious commitments or taking relationships to the next level.

On October 14th, the opposition between Venus in Sagittarius and Uranus in Taurus brings exciting and unexpected encounters in love. This aspect can lead to sudden attractions or romantic opportunities that deviate from your usual preferences. Embrace these unexpected experiences, as they may bring about personal growth and an expanded understanding of love.

The trine between Venus and Mars on October 8th ignites passion and enhances your physical and emotional connection with your partner. This aspect encourages sensual and intimate experiences, deepening the bond between you. It's a time to explore your desires and express your love with passion and enthusiasm.

For single Scorpios, the biquintile aspect between Venus and the True Node on October 22nd presents an opportunity for transformative romantic encounters. This alignment may bring someone into your life who aligns with your soul's purpose and supports your personal growth and spiritual journey.

However, it's important to remain mindful of the sesquiquadrate between Venus in Scorpio and Neptune in Pisces on October 3rd. This aspect can bring heightened sensitivity and idealism, potentially leading to unrealistic expectations or illusions in love. Maintain clear communication and ensure that your romantic pursuits are grounded in reality.

Career

In the career realm, October 2024 presents both challenges and opportunities for Scorpios. The astrological aspects influence your professional endeavors and emphasize the need for adaptability and strategic decision-making.

The quincunx aspect between Mercury in Scorpio and Saturn in Pisces on October 27th requires you to make adjustments in your approach to work. This alignment encourages you to find a balance between your ambitions and the practical demands of your career. It may involve reassessing your long-term goals and considering alternative paths to achieve success.

The opposition between Mercury in Scorpio and Uranus in Taurus on October 31st brings unexpected changes and breakthroughs in your professional life. This aspect can lead to innovative ideas, sudden opportunities, or unexpected challenges that require quick thinking and adaptability. Embrace the element of surprise and trust in your ability to handle unforeseen situations.

The sextile between Mars in Cancer and Uranus in Taurus on October 24th energizes your drive and creativity in the workplace. This aspect supports taking calculated risks and pursuing unique approaches to achieve your professional goals. It's a favorable time to assert your individuality and make bold moves that set you apart from the crowd.

The sesquiquadrate between Mercury in Scorpio and Jupiter in Gemini on October 17th emphasizes the importance of effective communication and networking in your career. This aspect encourages you to expand your professional connections, seek opportunities for collaboration, and share your ideas with confidence. Networking events, conferences, or social gatherings related to your field can be particularly fruitful during this time.

Finance

October 2024 brings a mix of favorable and challenging aspects in the realm of finances for Scorpios. It's essential to approach your financial matters with caution and make informed decisions.

The trine between Venus in Scorpio and Saturn in Pisces on October 4th supports your financial stability and encourages responsible money management. This aspect favors long-term investments and savings plans. It's a good time to review your financial goals and establish a solid foundation for your future.

The opposition between Venus in Sagittarius and Uranus in Taurus on October 14th can introduce unexpected financial opportunities or expenditures. Be cautious with impulsive spending and ensure that any financial decisions align with your long-term financial objectives. Exercise prudence and consider seeking professional advice before making major financial commitments.

The biquintile aspect between Venus and the True Node on October 22nd brings auspicious financial alignments. This alignment may lead to serendipitous financial encounters or opportunities that align with your life's purpose. Remain open to synchronicities and trust your intuition when it comes to financial matters.

The sesquiquadrate between Venus in Scorpio and Mars in Cancer on October 27th requires caution in financial partnerships or shared resources. This aspect can create tension or power struggles related to joint financial endeavors. Maintain clear boundaries and open communication to ensure equitable outcomes.

Health

In October 2024, the astrological aspects influence your health and well-being as a Scorpio. It's essential to prioritize self-care and maintain a balanced approach to your physical and emotional well-being.

The quincunx aspect between the Sun in Scorpio and Neptune in Pisces on October 20th highlights the need for discernment and moderation in your health routines. This alignment reminds you to be aware of potential escapism or indulgence that can affect your overall well-being. Finding a balance between rest and productivity is crucial during this period.

The sesquiquadrate between Mercury in Scorpio and Neptune in Pisces on October 21st emphasizes the importance of mental and emotional self-care. This aspect can bring heightened sensitivity or confusion, affecting your ability to focus and make sound decisions. Engage in practices such as meditation, journaling, or therapy to nurture your emotional well-being and maintain mental clarity.

The square between Mercury in Scorpio and Pluto in Capricorn on October 13th highlights the potential for power struggles or intense emotions that may impact your health. It's crucial to find healthy outlets for stress and manage any conflicts or emotional burdens. Engaging in physical activities such as yoga, jogging, or dancing can help release tension and promote overall well-being.

The opposition between the Sun in Scorpio and Chiron in Aries on October 13th emphasizes the need for self-compassion and healing. This aspect may bring to the surface past wounds or emotional triggers that impact your well-being. Take time for self-reflection, engage in self-care practices, and seek support from loved ones or professionals if needed.

Remember to listen to your body's needs and establish healthy routines that promote balance and vitality. Maintaining a nutritious diet, staying hydrated, and getting regular exercise are fundamental pillars of your well-being. Prioritize quality sleep and give yourself permission to rest and rejuvenate when necessary.

Travel

October 2024 presents favorable opportunities for Scorpios to embark on transformative journeys and explore new horizons. The astrological aspects indicate that travel can serve as a catalyst for personal growth and self-discovery.

The biquintile aspect between Venus and the True Node on October 21st encourages you to align your travel plans with your higher purpose. This alignment may bring about serendipitous encounters or experiences that contribute to your spiritual growth and personal evolution.

The sesquiquadrate between Venus in Scorpio and Neptune in Pisces on October 15th adds a touch of idealism and sensitivity to your travel experiences. It's essential to maintain realistic expectations and exercise caution while exploring unfamiliar territories. Trust your intuition and embrace a sense of wonder as you navigate new cultures and environments.

The trine between Venus in Scorpio and Mars in Cancer on October 8th enhances your travel experiences, promoting harmony and enjoyment during your journeys. This aspect suggests that activities such as romantic getaways, nature retreats, or group adventures can be particularly fulfilling during this time.

When planning your travels, consider destinations that align with your interests and aspirations. Whether you seek spiritual growth, adventure, or cultural immersion, choose locations that resonate with your soul's desires. Engaging with local communities, trying new cuisines, and exploring historical sites can provide enriching experiences.

However, it's important to remain mindful of potential disruptions or unexpected changes, given the quincunx aspect between the Sun in Libra and Uranus in Taurus on October 19th. Stay flexible in your travel plans and have contingency arrangements in place to navigate any unforeseen circumstances.

Insight from the stars

The astrological aspects in October 2024 indicate a period of profound transformation and personal growth for Scorpios. The combination of intense emotions, deep connections, and the drive for success creates a powerful energy for self-discovery and empowerment.

The aspects encourage you to embrace change, trust your instincts, and navigate through challenges with resilience. This transformative phase holds immense potential for personal evolution and fulfillment. By engaging in self-reflection, maintaining emotional balance, and pursuing your passions with unwavering determination, you can harness the cosmic energies to manifest positive changes in various aspects of your life.

Best days of the month: October 8th, 14th, 22nd, 24th, 28th, and 31st

November 2024

Horoscope

November 2024 brings a transformative and dynamic energy for Scorpios, influenced by the astrological aspects. This month presents opportunities for growth, deep emotional connections, and powerful self-discovery. As the Sun moves through Scorpio, you are encouraged to embrace your inner strength and navigate the depths of your emotions with courage and resilience.

The sextile between Jupiter in Gemini and Chiron in Aries on November 2nd offers opportunities for personal growth and healing. This aspect invites you to explore new perspectives and expand your understanding of yourself and the world around you.

Mercury's trine with Mars on November 2nd enhances your communication skills and intellectual pursuits. This alignment supports assertiveness and effective expression, empowering you to articulate your thoughts and ideas with clarity and confidence.

The opposition between Mars in Cancer and Pluto in Capricorn on November 3rd brings intensity and potential power struggles in your relationships and career. This aspect encourages you to confront any underlying issues and transform them into sources of personal empowerment.

Love

In November 2024, love takes on a transformative and passionate tone for Scorpios, influenced by the astrological aspects. This month offers opportunities for deep emotional connections, personal growth, and profound experiences in your relationships.

The opposition between Venus in Sagittarius and Jupiter in Gemini on November 3rd may bring contrasting desires and perspectives within your relationships. This aspect encourages open and honest communication to bridge any gaps and foster understanding. It's important to find a balance between personal freedom and the need for connection, allowing space for individual growth while nurturing the bonds with your partner.

On the same day, Venus forms a trine with Chiron in Aries, creating an atmosphere of healing and growth within your love life. This aspect invites you to explore vulnerability and express your deepest emotions with your partner. It's a time to embrace your emotional wounds, share your vulnerabilities, and create a safe space for emotional intimacy.

The sesquiquadrate between the Sun in Scorpio and Neptune in Pisces on November 4th may heighten your sensitivity and idealism in love. This aspect calls for clarity and discernment to avoid potential illusions or unrealistic expectations. Remain grounded in reality while maintaining a compassionate and empathetic approach to your relationships.

The trine between the Sun in Scorpio and Saturn in Pisces on November 4th brings stability and commitment to your love life. This aspect supports long-term relationships and offers a solid foundation for mutual growth and shared responsibilities. It's a time to deepen your commitment and build a secure and enduring partnership.

The biquintile between Venus and Uranus on November 12th encourages spontaneity and excitement in love. This aspect may bring unexpected encounters or romantic opportunities that deviate from your usual preferences. Embrace the element of surprise and be open to exploring new dimensions of love and relationships.

For single Scorpios, the opposition between Venus in Sagittarius and Jupiter in Gemini on November 3rd can inspire you to broaden your horizons and engage in new social experiences. This alignment encourages you to step outside your comfort zone, meet new people, and embrace diverse perspectives in your search for love.

Career

November 2024 presents both opportunities and challenges in the career sphere for Scorpios. The astrological aspects influence your professional endeavors, encouraging you to take calculated risks and embrace transformative changes.

The trine between Mercury in Scorpio and Mars in Cancer on November 2nd enhances your assertiveness and drive in the workplace. This alignment empowers you to pursue your career goals with passion and determination, inspiring those around you.

On November 12th, the square between Mercury in Sagittarius and Saturn in Pisces may bring obstacles or delays in your career progression. This aspect urges you to exercise patience, maintain discipline, and approach challenges with a strategic mindset. By persevering, you can overcome setbacks and achieve long-term success.

The opposition between Mercury in Sagittarius and Jupiter in Gemini on November 18th encourages open-mindedness and a broader perspective in your professional pursuits. This aspect inspires you to embrace new ideas, seek intellectual growth, and consider alternative approaches to problem-solving.

Finance

November 2024 holds mixed influences for Scorpio's finances, prompting careful consideration and strategic decision-making. The astrological aspects indicate the need for financial planning and mindful spending.

The opposition between Venus in Sagittarius and Jupiter in Gemini on November 3rd may bring conflicting desires when it comes to your financial goals. It's important to find a balance between enjoying the present moment and saving for the future. Seek wise counsel and consider long-term financial strategies before making major financial commitments.

The quincunx aspect between Venus in Capricorn and Mars in Leo on November 14th may create tension or challenges related to your financial partnerships or shared resources. This alignment encourages you to maintain clear communication, establish boundaries, and ensure equitable outcomes in joint financial endeavors.

The square between Venus in Capricorn and Uranus in Taurus on November 9th suggests the potential for unexpected financial disruptions or expenses. It's crucial to have a contingency plan and remain adaptable to navigate through any unforeseen financial circumstances.

Health

In terms of health, November 2024 prompts Scorpios to prioritize self-care and emotional well-being. The astrological aspects influence your physical vitality and emotional balance, urging you to nurture both aspects of your well-being.

The sesquiquadrate between the Sun in Scorpio and Neptune in Pisces on November 4th emphasizes the importance of maintaining clear boundaries and discernment in your emotional and energetic interactions. This aspect reminds you to distinguish between your own emotions and those of others, protecting your energy and preserving emotional balance.

The trine between the Sun in Scorpio and Saturn in Pisces on November 4th offers stability and discipline in your health routines. This aspect encourages you to establish healthy habits, practice self-discipline, and adhere to structured wellness regimens.

The opposition between the Sun in Scorpio and Uranus in Taurus on November 16th may bring unexpected disruptions or changes in your health. It's essential to remain adaptable and seek balance amidst any unforeseen circumstances. Engage in stress-reducing activities, prioritize rest, and maintain a well-rounded approach to your physical and emotional well-being.

Travel

November 2024 presents opportunities for transformative travel experiences for Scorpios. The astrological aspects influence your journeys, promoting personal growth, and expanding your horizons.

The biquintile aspect between Venus and Uranus on November 12th encourages you to embrace spontaneity and explore unconventional travel destinations or experiences. This alignment sparks a sense of adventure and offers unique encounters that broaden your perspective.

The sesquiquadrate between Venus in Capricorn and Mars in Leo on November 14th suggests the need for careful planning and organization in your travel arrangements. This aspect reminds you to pay attention to details and logistics to ensure a smooth and enjoyable journey.

Consider destinations that offer opportunities for self-reflection, spiritual growth, or cultural exploration. Whether it's a meditation retreat, historical city, or natural wonder, choose places that resonate with your interests and desires.

Insight from the stars

November 2024 indicates a transformative period of growth and self-discovery for Scorpios. By embracing deep emotional connections, taking calculated risks in your career, and finding balance in your finances, you can navigate this month with grace and resilience. Remember to prioritize your physical and emotional well-being, engaging in self-care practices and maintaining clear boundaries. Trust in the transformative power of your experiences and the wisdom of the stars as you continue to evolve on your personal journey.

Best days of the month: November 2nd, 12th, 18th, 20th, 24th, 27th, and 30th

December 2024

Horoscope

December 2024 brings a mix of transformative energies and opportunities for growth for Scorpios, influenced by the astrological aspects. This month encourages you to delve deep into your emotions, reflect on the past year, and prepare for a new chapter of self-discovery and personal evolution.

The biquintile aspect between Venus and Jupiter on December 1st infuses your relationships with optimism and a sense of expansion. This alignment fosters harmony and encourages you to embrace joy and abundance within your connections.

Mercury's trine with Chiron on December 2nd supports healing and growth in your communication. This aspect empowers you to express your emotions and engage in conversations that bring understanding and empathy to your relationships.

As Venus trines Uranus on December 2nd, exciting and unexpected romantic opportunities may present themselves. This alignment encourages you to embrace new experiences and explore unique paths to love and connection.

Love

In December 2024, love takes on a transformative and introspective tone for Scorpios, influenced by the astrological aspects. This month offers opportunities for deep emotional connections, self-reflection, and the exploration of profound love experiences.

The biquintile aspect between Venus and Jupiter on December 1st infuses your love life with a sense of optimism and expansion. This alignment encourages you to embrace the abundance of love and joy available to you. It's a time to open your heart to new possibilities, whether you are single or in a relationship.

On December 2nd, Mercury forms a trine with Chiron, creating a supportive environment for healing and growth in your romantic connections. This aspect invites you to engage in heartfelt conversations, express your emotions, and explore vulnerable aspects of your relationships. Honest communication can foster a deeper understanding and strengthen the bonds with your partner.

The trine between Venus in Capricorn and Uranus in Taurus on December 2nd brings unexpected and exciting romantic opportunities your way. This alignment encourages you to embrace spontaneity and embrace the thrill of new connections. Be open to unconventional experiences and allow love to unfold in surprising ways.

The square between Venus in Aquarius and Mars in Leo on December 12th creates a dynamic and passionate energy in your love life. This aspect ignites your desire and intensifies the connection with your partner. It's a time to embrace passion, explore your deepest desires, and express your affection boldly.

Career

December 2024 presents opportunities for professional growth and progress for Scorpios. The astrological aspects influence your career sector, inspiring you to pursue your goals with determination and strategic thinking.

The opposition between Mercury in Sagittarius and Jupiter in Gemini on December 4th may bring conflicting ideas or beliefs in your professional endeavors. This aspect encourages you to consider multiple perspectives and engage in open dialogue to find creative solutions. Avoid overextending yourself and maintain focus on your long-term goals.

The square between the Sun in Sagittarius and Saturn in Pisces on December 4th may present challenges or delays in your career path. This aspect reminds you to remain patient and disciplined, adhering to your responsibilities and working diligently to overcome obstacles.

The biquintile aspect between Mars and Saturn on December 4th brings a harmonious blend of ambition and discipline to your career pursuits. This alignment supports strategic planning, consistent effort, and a methodical approach to achieving your professional objectives.

Finance

In terms of finances, December 2024 prompts Scorpios to exercise caution and engage in practical decision-making. The astrological aspects influence your financial sector, highlighting the importance of budgeting, long-term planning, and careful consideration of investments.

The semi-square between Venus in Aquarius and Saturn in Pisces on December 5th may bring a need for restraint and discipline in your financial choices. This aspect encourages you to prioritize financial stability and make responsible decisions regarding your resources.

The square between Venus in Aquarius and Uranus in Taurus on December 28th may create unexpected financial disruptions or expenses. It's crucial to have a contingency plan and remain adaptable to navigate through any unforeseen financial circumstances.

Take time to review your financial goals and establish a solid foundation for future growth. Seek the advice of financial professionals if needed and avoid impulsive spending.

Health

December 2024 highlights the importance of self-care and balance in your physical and emotional well-being. The astrological aspects influence your health sector, urging you to prioritize rest, rejuvenation, and mindful practices.

The semi-square between the Sun and Venus on December 11th may bring a need for balance in your self-care routine. This aspect reminds you to attend to both your physical and emotional needs, finding harmony between work and relaxation.

The opposition between Venus in Aquarius and Mars in Leo on December 12th may create tension or conflicts between your desires for pleasure and the need for discipline in maintaining a healthy lifestyle. Strive for moderation and find a balance that allows you to enjoy the festive season while also nurturing your well-being.

Engage in stress-reducing activities, such as meditation, yoga, or spending time in nature. Prioritize quality sleep and nourishing meals to support your overall vitality.

Travel

December 2024 offers opportunities for meaningful travel experiences that broaden your horizons and deepen your understanding of the world. The astrological aspects influence your travel sector, encouraging exploration and cultural immersion.

The biquintile aspect between Venus and Jupiter on December 1st sparks a sense of adventure and inspires you to embark on journeys that expand your knowledge and worldview. Consider destinations that offer rich cultural experiences, historical significance, or spiritual enlightenment.

The square between Venus in Aquarius and Uranus in Taurus on December 28th may create unexpected changes or disruptions in your travel plans. It's advisable to have flexible itineraries and make necessary adjustments to accommodate unforeseen circumstances.

Embrace the opportunity to connect with people from different cultures, learn new languages, and immerse yourself in the local customs and traditions of the places you visit. Engage in mindful travel practices, respecting the environment and the communities you encounter.

Insight from the stars

The astrological aspects in December 2024 bring a blend of challenges and opportunities for Scorpios. By embracing transformative energies, fostering open communication, and maintaining a disciplined approach, you can navigate this month with resilience and growth. Remember to prioritize your physical and emotional well-being, make strategic decisions in your finances and career, and engage in meaningful travel experiences that broaden your perspective. Trust in the wisdom of the stars as you embrace the journey of self-discovery and prepare for the year ahead.

Best days of the month: December 2nd, 10th, 12th, 19th, 20th 23rd, and 31st.

Printed in Great Britain
by Amazon